GET A GRIP
ON YOUR MONEY

A Young Adult Study in
Christian Financial Management
TEACHER'S GUIDE

Larry Burkett

Focus on the Family Publishing
Pomona, California 91799

GET A GRIP ON YOUR MONEY, Teacher's Guide
© Copyright 1990 by Larry Burkett
All rights reserved.

The forms in this book may be reproduced for their intended educational purpose without permission from the publisher. They may not be used or reproduced in any other books having similar purpose, or resyndicated in part or in whole for resale without prior written permission from the publisher.

Except for brief excerpts for review purposes, no other part of this book may be reproduced or used in any form without written permission from Focus on the Family Publishing.

Printed in the United States of America
Edited by Dave and Neta Jackson

Larry Burkett
GET A GRIP ON YOUR MONEY, Teacher's Guide

Summary: Teacher's guide for a course on managing personal finances designed for teens' classroom use. Emphasis is on using Christian principles in budgeting, writing a resume', and applying for a job.

Focus on the Family Publishing
Rolf Zettersten, Vice President
Dean Merrill, Vice President, Communications
Wes Haystead, Curriculum Editor
Dave and Neta Jackson, Contributing Editors
Illustrations, David Slonim
Design, Jerry Price
ISBN 0-929608-74-7
90 91 92 93 94 95 / 10 9 8 7 6 5 4 3 2

CONTENTS

Introduction

Lessons:

Quiz Answers

INTRODUCTION

This study is designed for young people, ages fifteen through twenty. Its purpose is to teach them how to manage money (particularly through careful budgeting) and make the financial decisions they will face on their own as adults. All of the steps recommended in this course are based on biblical principles and solid financial experience.

The student book can be used in four ways:

1. As a basic course for a group study with a leader. It requires about an hour of work together per lesson.
2. As an advanced course in a class where students are expected to do an hour of homework ("For Additional Study") along with the hour of in-class work for each lesson. The homework is vital if you intend students to master the course concepts.
3. As a basic independent study that can be completed in about one hour of work per lesson.
4. As an advanced independent study going into greater depth and requiring up to two hours of work to complete the basic lesson and the "For Additional Study" at the end of each lesson.

This course uses a simulation method for learning how to manage money. It duplicates such conditions as paying taxes, buying homes, cars, clothes, and keeping a budget. In addition, the students will learn how to choose life insurance and what it means to pay simple or add-on interest, how to look for work, write a resume, and have a successful job interview.

If possible, classes should not exceed twenty students, and an assistant to the leader is very helpful for groups of ten or more in order to monitor each student's budgeting process.

Materials:

Besides this Teacher's Guide you will need a copy of the Student Text.

In the back of this Teacher's Guide you will find Forms and Resources that you will need to photocopy for the class. The number of copies of each Form that each student will need depends on whether you intend to teach the basic course or the advanced course (using the "For Additional Study" sections for homework). Use the Visual Masters to create transparencies for an overhead projector. You will need an overhead projector and a chalkboard for teaching this course.

The back of the Student Text also contains the reproducible

Forms, so students may duplicate additional copies for their work. The students should not use these masters for their work since they will need more than one copy of most forms.

The first column of "number of copies" (below) is for the basic course. The second column is for the advanced course.

Form Number	Title	Number of Copies	
		1 mo.	6 mo.
Form 1	Monthly Income and Expenses	4	4
Form 2	Division of Pay	2	2
Form 3	Individual Account Sheet	12	72
Form 4	Bank Deposits	1	3
Form 5	Blank Checks	10	60
Form 6	Checking Account Reconciliation	1	6
Form 7	Loan Applications	1	1
Form 8	Insurance Needs Worksheet	1	1
Form 9	Creating Your Resumé	1	1

Each student should use an inexpensive pocket calculator to do all the math computations for keeping a budget. While the arithmetic is simple, sharpening those skills is not the primary object of this course. On the other hand, error-free calculations are essential.

Each student will also need a folder in which to keep the various forms as he or she fills them out.

Resource Persons:

Several lessons recommend the use of an outside resource person who can speak to the class for a few minutes on the subject of the lesson. Begin to set up these appointments now:

    Lesson 6 a banker
    Lesson 7 a life insurance broker
    Lesson 10 a real estate agent
    Lesson 12 a personnel director

Turn to each of these lessons and discover what the outside resource person can contribute. Be sure you recruit only people who will give honest and helpful information to the students. Don't, for instance, invite an insurance broker who can only see a roomfull of potential customers.

Review Quizzes:

Most of the lessons have a simple quiz for students to use in reviewing their grasp of the main ideas. The answers are found in the back of this book and in the back of each Student Text.

This Is Your Life:

Although these lessons simulate future decisions for most students, the "This Is Your Life" section of each lesson will help them apply what they've learned in class to their present situations. They should keep all "This Is Your Life" work in a separate folder.

For Additional Study:

Each week students are to work on setting up a simulated budget, then they carry on the equivalent of six months of record keeping (one month per week). Appendix B and E both provide helpful guidance in this process. These tasks are vital in order for students to master the concepts involved in establishing and maintaining a budget. Time should be taken in each session to review what students have done to ensure they are correctly applying the principles of the course.

CHOOSING A CAREER

Background:

Many people feel that more money will solve their financial problems. As a result they may borrow, try to expand their credit or attempt get-rich-quick schemes. They may become discouraged and slack off in their present job, try to work two jobs, or—if they are married—insist that the family needs two wage earners. These efforts are seldom the real cure.

This course, *Get a Grip on Your Money*, emphasizes responsible money management as the first step in avoiding financial problems or solving them if they occur.

In this lesson, students will begin their budget simulations by randomly picking careers and salaries. There will undoubtedly be some objections to the disparity in incomes. Help them deal with their natural urge to think that more money is the best or only solution to having what they need. Your task is not to discourage initiative for advancement but to build a foundation of wise management no matter what the income level. The person who is unable to manage a small salary will not be better off with a larger income.

NOTE: The dollar figures used in the examples are based on national averages and may vary significantly from actual income and expense levels in your area. While it will be helpful for your students to discover the actual costs of living in your area, keep the emphasis on the process involved rather than the specific dollar amounts.

Lesson Aim:
- **To introduce students to the course and the simulated practice in adult money management.**
- **To assign each student a simulated career and help him or her make the initial budget decisions.**

Advance Preparation:

☐ Make sure you have at least one photocopy of Form 1, "Monthly Income and Expenses," for each student. The masters for all forms are in the back of this manual. You will save time if you make all the copies now that you will need. See the Introduction for the quantity of each form you will need for each student. (Masters are also in the back of the Student Text.)

☐ Photocopy Resource A, "Job Assignments," from the back of this Teacher's Guide. Cut apart the twenty job descriptions on the dotted lines. Fold them once, and have them ready in a basket or hat for the students to draw their job assignments. Two more job descriptions are in Appendix A of the Student Text. If you have more than twenty students, make two copies of Resource A, resulting in at least some students having the same careers.

☐ Make a transparency for your overhead projector from Visual 1, "Budget Percentages," found in the back of this book.

GETTING STARTED (10 minutes)

Begin the course by introducing yourself and briefly sharing one "dumb" financial decision you have made: a purchase, investment or budgeting choice that created problems for you. Your openness in admitting a mistake will make it easier for some students to ask questions about areas they do not understand. Your story will also communicate the point that errors in money management can have significant impact on many other areas of a person's life.

Ask, "How much money do you think you would need in order to avoid financial problems?" Write on the chalkboard the amounts suggested without comment. Then present this brief opening lecture:

In this country, except when there are major economic upheavals or when large industries collapse, there are only three things you must do to have all the money you need:

1. Get a good job,
2. Be a diligent worker, and
3. Manage your money wisely.

This course will help you learn how to do all three, but the emphasis will on money management—the place where most people fail.

To begin, notice that the course centers around all the money you NEED, not All the Money You WANT. At first you may be disappointed if you were dreaming about a big yacht or three months of skiing in the Alps every year.

But wait.

Isn't it better to have the money you need than to struggle to avoid bankruptcy and to keep bill collectors from turning off your heat or repossessing your car? Isn't it better than ending up in divorce court because you and your spouse were never able to work out your money problems?

This course uses a simulation method for learning how to manage money. Many universities use this method to train students in their future vocations. The purpose is to reproduce, as closely as possible, the actual conditions you will face later. In the area of finances, this involves paying taxes, buying homes, cars or clothes. You will plan and prepare a budget and select the right home to fit that budget. Also, you'll learn how to choose life insurance and what it means to pay simple or add-on interest when you buy a car.

Financial problems contribute to nearly 90 percent of all the divorces in America. Virtually none of those people thought financial problems would destroy their marriages. The vast majority made mistakes out of simple ignorance.

Conclude your introductory comments by explaining the class schedule and your expectations for what each student will be responsible to do (i.e., class participation, homework, etc.).

STEP 1
Choosing Your Job (20 minutes)

Objective: To assign each student a career and its associated salary, taxes, etc.

1. Let the students draw their job assignments (Resource A) from a hat or basket. Invite each one to share and comment on what they drew, what their income and taxes are, etc.

   They will quickly notice that there is a considerable range in incomes. The most highly paid job (the doctor) gets more than three times the monthly income of the lowest paid people.

2. Ask, "What do you think about some people getting a much higher salary than others? How do you think this will affect how well they can do in the course?"

   This recognition may inspire some students to get a good education and strive for a higher-paying career. However, point out that the salary differences in this course will have no influence on how each student will succeed in learning how to manage the income available.

   Take time to allow any feelings to be expressed about the different levels of income. Help the students to accept that each person's real-life income is different, too. The person's own choices and priorities and the family into which he or she was born are some factors which produce these variations. The objective for the class—and in life—is to learn to do the most with what each one has.

3. Explain how the twice-monthly "take-home" pay is calculated. The tax rates and dollar amounts for this course were estimated and then averaged. The federal, state and FICA (Social Security) taxes have been lumped together as one tax deduction.

   Have the students turn to Appendix A in the back of their Text for two examples of how taxes have been figured. The amounts were estimated. For example, the pilot with a $30,000 per year income will pay federal income tax at 18 percent. State tax is 5 percent, and FICA (Social Security) is 7 percent—for a total tax of 30 percent.

4. Have each student fill out the top of a copy of Form 1, "Monthly Income and Expenses," entering Job, Annual Income and Monthly Income (annual salary divided by twelve).

STEP 2
Determining Net Spendable Income (15 minutes)

Objective: For each student to calculate correctly his or her net spendable income (NSI).

1. Teach the following:

   Your budgeting each month will be based on your net spendable income (NSI). This is your monthly salary, less any charitable contributions and taxes.

   Most charitable contributions can be tax deductible at the time your income tax is calculated. The deduction is allowed for contributions given to a nonprofit charitable, religious, or educational group that meets government guidelines. "Tax deductible" means that the amount is subtracted from your gross (or total) income before you calculate your annual tax bill.

2. Ask, "Why do you think this is allowed?" As the students offer their ideas, be sure someone mentions that society encourages the practice of charitable giving because it often benefits the public good.

3. Tell the students that they may enter any amount in the "charitable contributions" category, but this is not required. (You may want to take a few minutes to discuss the practice of charitable giving. Ask, "What are the advantages of giving away part of your income? What are the disadvantages?")

4. Explain that taxes are not an option. They must enter the amount shown on their job assignment.

5. Have students subtract charitable contributions and taxes from their monthly income to determine their Net Spendable Income (NSI). Direct the students' attention to the example in the Student Text. Check to be sure everyone correctly calculates their NSI on their copy of Form 1.

STEP 3
Estimating Budget Percentages (15 minutes)

Objective: For students to select the percentage amounts that they wish to spend in each category, not exceeding 100 percent total.

1. Display Visual 1, "Budget Percentages," on the overhead

projector. Give this explanation:

> In order for a person's budget to balance, it is necessary to manage the amounts spent in each category. For there to be enough for food, one can't spend too much for entertainment, etc.
>
> The percentages on the overhead are helpful in suggesting what the average person might spend in each category so the total will not exceed 100 percent.

2. On scratch paper, have the students determine the percentages they wish to use. They are free to allocate a larger percentage to those areas they value most. However, they must subtract the same amount from other categories so that the total of all categories does not exceed 100 percent.

   Allow time for the students to make these decisions for themselves.

3. When they have completed this process, each student should calculate the dollar equivalent for each category. The "Sample Budget Percentages and Dollar Amounts" in the Student Text shows one way to do this. Again, they should add all the amounts to be sure that the total does not exceed their NSI. Share these comments:

   > In real life there may be some "givens" which will limit your choices at this point. For example, you may want to peg your housing costs at 30% of your income. However, when you calculate the dollar amount, you may find there is nothing available in that price range. When that happens, you will need to increase the proportion of your budget in that category and decrease it in others. That is the process you will be working through in later sessions as you confront some of the realities of making a budget work. Right now, you are simply setting up a framework so that later adjustments can be made intelligently and responsibly, not in desperation or on impulse.

   Students may need to make several adjustments on scratch paper until their totals "work."

4. Instruct students to save their concluding amounts for the next lesson. They will use these figures to make their lifestyle selections—what kind of house they will live in, what kind of car they will drive, etc.

FOR ADDITIONAL STUDY

For additional study, have the students do the following (which also appears in their Student Texts):

1. Interview one full-time wage earner who keeps an accurate budget and is willing to share about his or her spending patterns. Record how much (and the percentages of Net Spendable Income) he or she spends in categories 3—12 mentioned above (as closely as they compare). Also, note whether the person has any other significant categories and the amounts and percentages in them.

2. Study Appendix B, "Budget Needs," which includes the choices available to you for each budget category. This will help you make better-informed choices in the next lesson.

3. Identify three jobs that would interest you as a long-term career. Then from the help-wanted ads in a local newspaper, determine the current salary range for those jobs in your part of the country. List any factors (experience, academic degrees, licenses, etc.) which influence salary level.

This Is Your Life

Although the lessons simulate future decisions for most students, this section will help them apply in real life what they've learned in class. They should keep all "This Is Your Life" work in a separate folder. The following instructions appear in the Student Text.

Do you know how much money you now make in a year? How much you spend on clothes...pizza...gas and bus fare? Are you always out of money and having to borrow from friends?

In order to have the necessary facts to "have all the money you need" right now and help you set up a personal budget, do the following:

1. Estimate your personal monthly income from all sources—from job, parents, gifts, etc. (Multiply by twelve to see what your estimated yearly income is.)

2. Determine the money you have to spend each month (your Net Spendable Income) by subtracting any charitable gifts and any taxes that are withheld from your monthly earnings. (Look for federal, state, and FICA withholdings on a paycheck stub.)

3. Identify the budget categories for your current and desired expenditures (i.e., clothing, food, entertainment, transportation, savings, etc.). Estimate the percentages and amounts you want to spend in each category, making sure the totals do not exceed 100%.

4. If accurately estimating your income and expenses is hard to do, you need to keep track of all actual income you receive for one month, and all actual expenditures. Do this simply by keeping a notebook handy and recording income on one page and a running list of all money spent and for what on another page. (Sound like busy-work? Knowing where the money is going is vital when learning to manage your money.)

BALANCING YOUR BUDGET

Background:

Learning to balance a budget involves living within limits, making trade-offs between options. Some people resist keeping a budget because they think it is contrary to the carefree lifestyle they desire.

Just the opposite is true. Life is filled with limits and choices. The person who chooses to become a doctor can't get the required medical training while roaming the beaches of Australia. Every choice one makes closes other doors. When you spend your money on a new car, you probably won't have it for that vacation you want. Facing these facts of life is a required part of growing up.

Immaturity tries to avoid these facts, sometimes by not making a commitment to one career, one spouse, the affordable purchase, etc. In the financial arena, going into debt is one method of avoidance—buy the new car AND go on that expensive vacation—on credit. Yet sooner or later the piper must be paid. Only then does a person discover that the most care-filled, oppressive lifestyle is the one burdened down by excessive past debts.

This lesson helps the students learn how make those trade-off choices. Do they want a better house? Then they will have to accept a less-expensive car or a simpler vacation. Budget balancing does force one to make the hard choices, but the reward is freedom, the freedom of having the resources to afford the choice without worry.

Lesson Aim:
- **To guide the students in setting up a realistic budget to fit their individual salary range and paycheck frequency.**
- **To consider the factors that tempt people to try living beyond their income.**

Advance Preparation

☐ Make photocopies of Form 2, "Division of Pay," from the Student Text, one copy for each student.

☐ Make a transparency for your overhead projector from Visual 2, "Division of Pay," found in the back of this book.

☐ If you did not assign the "For Additional Study" from last lesson, find five or six job opportunities in interesting careers advertised in your local paper. Select ones that list salary range and special qualifications. Circle them in the newspaper and make a copy of each to distribute to five or six students. Call on them to share salary range and job qualifications during the Getting Started section of this lesson.

☐ Arrange your classroom so that you can have the students divide into groups of three for a portion of this lesson.

Getting Started (5 minutes)

If you assigned "For Additional Study" from the last lesson, invite three or four students to report what they discovered when they interviewed people who keep an accurate budget.

What were the amounts and percentages the interviewees spent in categories 3—12 on Form 1? (Of course, the categories of every budget may not correspond, but try to match them as closely as possible.)

Were there any other significant categories used by those interviewed?

Have several students report what they discovered about interesting careers from the help wanted ads in their local paper.

- The type of job.
- The salary range.
- Any special qualifications required and how they might influence salary.

STEP 1
Making Choices within Your Budget Categories (20 minutes)

Objective: For the students to make specific choices within their budget categories based on the amounts they determined they could spend in each category.

1. Instruct the students to divide into groups of three. Then have them take out the calculations they did during the last session (the dollar amounts they calculated for each of the categories on Form 1, "Monthly Income and Expenses").

2. Tell the students to select from Appendix B ("Budget Needs" in the Student Text) one budget item from each category 3—12. They are then to list the corresponding numbers and amounts on their copy of Form 1.

    For housing and auto selections, they can only choose purchases for which they have sufficient down payments. The "cash" they have saved was designated with their job assignment from session one.

    For those categories where no options are given (food, savings, medical), they should use the percentage/dollar amounts they calculated from their NSI.

    Encourage the students to work together in making their selections, discussing what they want, what they can afford, and how they will reconcile the two. As they work, move among them, monitoring their progress and asking them to explain their choices.

    They can refer to Step 1 in the Student Text for an example

of what a completed Form 1 should look like.

STEP 2
Adjustments (15 minutes)

Objective: To allow the students to adjust their estimated category amounts to reflect the best choices among their options.

In some instances the dollar amount that some of the students designated for particular categories will not buy what they need or want in that category. Yet possibly for another $20 per month they could get the house they want. This is the time to adjust.

1. Instruct students that when they face a shortfall in a category, they will need to make a decision: lower their expectations or transfer money from some other category. Encourage the students to continue interacting with each other during this process.

2. Finally, when they think everything fits within their budget, they should do a final sum of all the category amounts to see if the total remains within their NSI.

   The bottom line is: their budget must balance!

3. Disband the small groups of three, and have the class reunite. Lead a general discussion of what might have influenced their budget decisions if they were making real-life choices. Call upon various students, asking:

   > What house did you choose?
   > What is its description?
   > Do you think you would be satisfied living in such a house?
   > Is the "image" of a more luxurious house a temptation for you? Why or why not?

4. Ask similar questions about car purchases, entertainment and recreation, and clothing budget.

5. Ask if anyone is saving more or less than 5 percent and why.

   One reminder: except for Category 7 (Debt), everyone must budget something for each category. They will be required to handle expenses in each category throughout this course.

6. Allow a few minutes for students to make any final adjustments in their budget. This is their last chance.

STEP 3
Locking in Your Budget (5 minutes)

Objective: To record their budget in its final form.

With the various changes, it is likely that the students' working copies of Form 1, "Monthly Income and Expenses," are somewhat of a mess. Therefore, have them copy their final budgets onto fresh copies of Form 1.

STEP 4
Division of Pay (10 minutes)

Objective: To explain how various pay periods require allocation of each check differently to meet all expenses when they come due.

1. Call on volunteers to tell how often they (if they work at a regular job) or their parents get paid. Have the students tell how many paychecks would be received in a year for each frequency. List each variation on the chalkboard until all the following are mentioned.

    - Weekly 52/yr.
    - Every two weeks 26/yr.
    - Twice per month 24/yr.
    - Monthly 12/yr.

    NOTE: When a person gets paid in any way other than monthly, they must determine how they will divide their pay to cover their expenses during that month.
    This course assumes a twice-monthly paycheck.

2. Therefore, each student will need to divide his or her expenses so that the payments are balanced. Half the expenses should be paid in the beginning of the month and the other half near the end. Of course some expenses, like food, are more consistent throughout the month. So the students must spend some for food in each half.

    Using a copy of Form 2, "Division of Pay," from the Student Text, have the students divide their allocation of pay so that their payments and income balance.

    Display Visual 2, "Division of Pay." It is an example of how someone with a $30,000 per year income might divide his or her expenses.

    The housing allowance has been taken out of the first paycheck. This is because house payments are most commonly due before the fifteenth of the month, which is the next pay period. To meet this large payment, the example shifts most of the car allocation, insurance, entertainment, clothing, etc., to the second pay period.

    This payment schedule is something to keep in mind when negotiating a car loan. The buyer might need to arrange the payment date for the sixteenth or later.

STEP 5
Calculating Irregular Expenses (5 minutes)

Objective: To demonstrate how irregular expenses are calculated and saved for.

1. Explain to the students that irregular or non-monthly expenses are handled in a different way. In their budget the irregular expenses such as vacations, dentist, doctor, etc., have been allocated monthly by percentage. In real life, it doesn't always work out that neatly. Someone may be overspending without knowing it, because they have no vacation budget.

2. Ask, "What are they likely to do when they want to take off for the Rocky Mountains or the Bahamas and there's no money reserved for that purpose?" (Too often they feel that because they've been working so hard they deserve a vacation, so they charge much of the cost on their credit cards. However, when the bills come in, they are difficult to pay.)

3. Explain that the way to avoid this problem is to estimate how much one expects to spend in an area. Then divide that total by twelve to arrive at the monthly average. Better yet, if records have been kept for the past year, those should be used as a more realistic source for estimating the annual cost.

   Show how to determine the monthly amounts, putting examples on the chalkboard, or referring the students to the example under Step 5 in the Student Text.

This Is Your Life

Applying what they've learned to their present finances. The following appears in the Student Text.

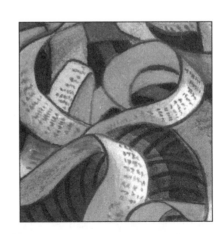

1. Have you recorded your actual income and expenditures during the past week? Continue keeping track in your personal notebook. Remember, the goal is to list all actual income and spending for a full month.

2. Using a copy of Form 1 ("Monthly Income and Expenses") as a guide, list your estimated monthly income, charitable contributions, taxes, and Net Spendable Income at the top. (The results from "This Is Your Life," Lesson 1.) Then make a list of the real expense categories you normally face in a month. Include Food, Fun, Transportation, School, Clothes, Savings, Miscellaneous, etc. (Don't try to figure percentages or fill in amounts—that will come later.)

3. If you have a job, how often do you receive a paycheck? Fill out an extra copy of Form 2, "Division of Pay." What does each

paycheck usually get spent for? (Do you spend paycheck #1 and save #2? Are you always out of money and having to borrow from parents and friends—then spend your paychecks paying people back? Be honest!)

4. Think ahead. What irregular expenses pop up during a year: summer activities? special clothes or equipment for sports? school clothes in September? How do you usually meet those needs financially? (Do your parents kick in? Do you get an extra job, go in debt, use your savings?)

FOR ADDITIONAL STUDY

For additional study, have the students do the following (which appears in their Student Texts). If you assign item 2, be sure to supply extra copies of Form 1, "Monthly Income and Expenses."

1. Ask your parents or someone else if you can review their bills for electricity or heat for the last year. Usually, these will vary from month to month because of fluctuations in the weather. Record the bills for each month, then establish the average monthly cost. (Some utility companies allow their established customers to pay equal monthly payments throughout the year so that costs don't fluctuate drastically.)

2. Suppose you have charged a $1,130 vacation on your MasterCard and a new bedroom set for $1,300 at Sears. Your combined monthly payments on these debts equals $90. (Charge card interest rates are usually very high. The monthly payment above is calculated at 19.8 percent annual interest over a three-year repayment period.) On a fresh copy of Form 1, "Monthly Income and Expenses," recalculate your categories.
   a. First fill in $90 under Category 7.
   b. Figure its percentage of your NSI. (If your NSI was $1,500, the equation would be $90 ÷ $1,500 = 6%).
   c. Reduce other category percentages to allow for this percentage. (For instance, if your debt equals 6 percent, you will need to reduce one or more categories by a total of that many percentage points.)
   d. Recalculate the dollar value for each category you have changed.
   e. Check to see that your percentages total 100 percent and that the dollar value of all categories does not exceed your NSI.
   f. Decide what spending changes you will make to remain within that amount. Will you have to live in a less costly house, cut back on entertainment and recreation, or what?

Notice how the implications of debt affect your freedom in other areas. Also, you might be interested in knowing that besides repaying your debt, you would have to pay an additional $810 in interest on these purchases before you were debt-free. Can you think of better things to do with that money?

SETTING UP YOUR RECORDS

Background:

Merely having enough money in the bank to make a desired purchase isn't the only criteria for staying out of debt. One objective of a good budget is to reserve funds for all necessary expenses. However, you lose this advantage if you spend those reserves for undesignated expenditures.

Many of the designated categories are essential—one has to pay the rent or mortgage and buy food. If the money isn't there when the time comes, it will have to be borrowed. The person is thrown into debt just as surely as if the money had been borrowed for the "desired purchase" in the beginning.

This is why any effective budget must show the money available by category.

Lesson Aim:
- To practice using individual account records as a means of managing funds within a budget category.
- To practice using a checking account along with the individual accounts.

Advance Preparation:

☐ Prepare transparency, Visual 3, "Individual Account Sheet."
For each student:
   ☐ make twelve copies of Form 3, "Individual Account Sheet";
   ☐ one copy of Form 4, "Bank Deposits";
   ☐ ten copies of Form 5, "Blank Checks."

Getting Started (5 minutes)

Begin the class by sharing the following example (printed in the Student Text):

> Suppose you are trying to decide whether you can afford a new TV. The local discount appliance store is having a "midnight madness sale," and the new Motorola that you want is on sale for $239.95. Things have been going well. You've paid the mortgage this month and are up to date on all your other bills and still have $289.32 in your checking account.
>   Should you do it?

Invite class members to suggest what they might do, then ask them to identify any other factors they feel should be considered. Next, continue with the example.

> At first it looks good. Then you remember that some of your accumulated funds initially had other purposes. For two months you haven't had any medical expenses—that accounts for $150. Your miscellaneous expenses haven't been as high as you anticipated, so you've saved money there, but then there's that vacation for which you were saving. Part of the money should go for it. But how much?

One of the benefits of budgeting is the ability to know when you can afford something and when you can't. It's great to be able to make a purchase without worrying whether you'll have enough for other needs.

Using individual account sheets is the key to this freedom. If it were practical (and safe), you could hold all your money in cash, putting the prescribed amounts in different envelopes. Then, by looking in your "Miscellaneous" envelope, you would know whether you had an extra $239.95 for that new TV.

Ask the students if they can think of another way to accomplish the same thing without using envelopes.

STEP 1
Individual Account Sheets *(15 minutes)*

Objective: To have the students open an individual account for each budget category except taxes.

1. Distribute twelve copies of Form 3, the "Individual Account Sheet," to each student. Explain the purpose of these sheets:

   Since it isn't safe to keep hundreds of dollars in envelopes in your home, you will want to put most of each paycheck in the bank. You can safely pay bills by check.

   Individual account sheets can do the same thing as envelopes of cash. You deposit the money in an account (on paper) for each category (housing, food, auto, etc.) and then withdraw it as needed. The account sheets show you how much is there at any one time by recording how much is put in and how much is taken out. The total amount shown on all the account sheets equals the total amount in the checking account.

   You should never spend based on your checking account balance. Rather, spend by category, based on the individual account sheet. If the "Miscellaneous" individual account sheet says there is an extra $239.95 of miscellaneous money, then it is possible to purchase that TV without worrying about a shortfall somewhere else. This discipline brings considerable freedom of mind.

2. Show how to use the individual account sheets, beginning with one for housing. Assume there is a NSI of $1,500 and a housing allotment of $420.

   Display Visual 3, "Individual Account Sheet," keeping a sheet of paper under the transparency so that only the heading shows on the screen. Then explain the following steps.

First: The information at the top is filled in—the name of the category ("Housing"); the monthly allocation ($420 in this case); the amount applied to this category from the first paycheck ($420); and the amount applied from the second pay period ($0).

The entire $420 allocation comes out of the first pay period because the mortgage must be paid near the beginning of the month. This was determined by Form 2, "Division of Pay," from the previous lesson.

Second: (Slide the paper mask down under the transparency to reveal the first filled-in line of the ledger.) When the first paycheck arrives and is deposited in the bank, a deposit is likewise made on the housing individual account sheet. The entry includes the date (1-1 for January 1), the amount of the "deposit," and the balance. This shows that there is $420 available to spend on housing this month.

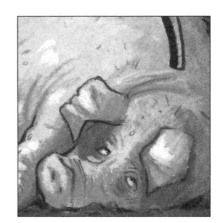

Third: (Remove the paper mask completely to display the full transparency.) Pay the bills as they come due, up to the $420 allotment. Each time a check is written, record it on the appropriate individual account sheet and calculate the resulting balance.

NOTE: The category balance declines with every check written. This shows exactly how much is left to spend, just as an envelope containing cash would do.

NOTE: The next deposit to this account doesn't occur until the first pay period of the next month. Other categories, such as food and auto, receive deposits twice a month according to the plan established by the division of pay.

3. Refer the students to the end of Step 1 in the Student Text for an illustration of how Form 1 ("Monthly Income and Expenses") was the source of information for filling out Form 2 ("Division of Pay"). This in turn tells how much goes into each category's Individual Account Sheet (Form 3).

4. Have the students fill out the top of a copy of Form 3, "Individual Account Sheet," for each category, 1—12 (except taxes). They should also write the amount of their initial deposit and balance in each category (the first line of the ledger).

STEP 2
Using a Checking Account (15 minutes)

Objective: To have students create their checkbook ledger.

1. Ask, "What do you think are the major problems people encounter in using a checking account?" Guide your class members to identify the following common problems experienced by about half of all check writers:

   - They make errors.
   - They can only guess at how much they have in their accounts.
   - They are never able to balance their checkbook.
   - Many people pay overdraft charges of $10 per check (or more) and develop a bad reputation with merchants who have been given bad checks.
   - Some people have been arrested for writing checks when they have insufficient funds to cover them.
   - Even when legal prosecution doesn't ensue, the hassle and embarrassment are considerable.

   These problems show why using a checking account properly is so important.

2. Explain that since you can't provide an actual checkbook, the students will need to create their own checkbook ledger using a copy of Form 3, "Individual Account Sheet."

3. Distribute one copy of Form 4, "Bank Deposits," and ten copies of Form 5, "Blank Checks," to each student. Have the students take a few moments to number each check sequentially, starting with #100.

4. Then, at the top of their last Form 3, have the students:

   - Write "Checkbook Ledger" for the account name.
   - Enter the amount of their twice-monthly paycheck in the first and second pay periods. (The amount of each paycheck was shown on the job description they drew in Lesson 1.)
   - Add the two together to fill in the monthly allocation.

   Refer the students to Step 2 in the Student Text for an example of a checkbook ledger. This example represents a month's records of someone who took home two paychecks per month of $875 each. (It does not include the check-writing charges which will be discussed in the next lesson.)

STEP 3
Integrating Account Sheets and Checkbook Ledger (10 minutes)

Objective: To show how the individual account sheets must be integrated with the checkbook ledger.

1. Explain the purpose of the two separate records:

> In order to know how much is available in each category, it is necessary to maintain two separate records.
> - One (the checkbook ledger) tells the total amount in the checking account.
> - The other (your individual account sheets) tell how much is left in each category of the budget.
>
> For instance, although there may be $289.32 in the checking account, that doesn't mean $239.95 of it can be freely used for a new TV. Other bills may still need to be paid.

2. Ask, "If I write a check, where must I record what I did?" (It must be posted in the checkbook ledger and the proper individual account sheet.) Point out the examples in the Student Text which illustrate this.

> **NOTE:** The examples show that on 1-1 (January 1) a deposit and four checks were recorded in the checkbook ledger. The deposit ($875) was divided among the various categories as predetermined on Form 2, "Division of Pay," from the last lesson. Then check #101 was recorded on the individual account sheet for charitable giving (category 1).
>
> In the checkbook ledger a circled (1) was written next to the transaction to signify that the individual account sheet for that category has been updated.
>
> Similarly, check #102 was recorded on the housing individual account sheet (category 3), and a circled (3) was written in the checkbook ledger. Each check was recorded on the proper individual account sheet.

3. Summarize this process by emphasizing that after updating all the categories, the total of the remaining funds in all categories on all the individual account sheets should equal the balance in the checkbook ledger.

STEP 4
Putting It Into Practice *(15 minutes)*

Objective: To begin proper recording of deposits and checks.

At this point the students should have filled out the heading on eleven individual account sheets—one for each category except taxes. They also should have filled out the heading of another individual account sheet as their checkbook ledger.

Now guide them through the following steps to start a month's record keeping. If they get lost, they can find the list under Step 4 of the Student Text.

1. Fill out a "Bank Deposit" slip (Form 4) for one paycheck.
2. Record that deposit in the checkbook ledger. Be sure to include the date and balance.
3. Divide that amount into categories by entering a "deposit" for each category on the individual account sheets.
4. Write one check each for categories 1 (if they are going to give anything), 3, 4 (one fourth of their monthly food allocation), 8, and 9. Make up the names of the companies receiving payment (e.g., "National Mortgage" for a housing payment, "Big Star Foods" for the grocery store). See Appendix E for guidance.
5. Record all checks in the checkbook ledger and calculate the running balances.
6. Record all payments on the individual account sheets.
7. Add up all the balances from the individual account sheets, and compare the figure to the checkbook ledger balance. If the amounts are the same, it should be correct. Otherwise, they should review their calculations to locate the error.

Circulate through the class, helping where needed, and seeing that the students start their accounting correctly.

This Is Your Life

Applying what they've learned to their present finances. The following appears in the Student Text.

1. Two weeks down—two weeks to go! Continue recording in your personal notebook all money in (income) and all money out (expenditures) for one month.
2. Using your "personalized" copy of Form 1, with the list you made of real spending categories (Food, Fun, Clothes, etc.), estimate what percentage of your Net Spendable Income (NSI) you'd like to spend in each category. Remember, the total

percentages must add up to 100 percent. Now calculate what amount of your NSI each percentage would be.

3. Using extra copies of Form 3, "Individual Account Sheets," fill in the name of each real spending category (one category per sheet). Save for use later.

4. Is your monthly income over $100? If so, consider opening a checking account. Keep a portion of your income as cash for miscellaneous expenses; pay for others (such as clothes) with a check.

FOR ADDITIONAL STUDY

If you assigned item 2 from the "For Additional Study" from last lesson, collect the alternative Form 1 from each student. If you have time, discuss how they adjusted their budget to meet the debt and how they feel about buying on credit.

It is important that students practice using the checkbook ledger and individual account sheets. Instruct them to write another eight to twelve checks, using at least three or four different categories. Appendix E provides helpful examples. They are to make sure that the balance in the checkbook ledger equals the total of the balances on the individual account sheets.

Have the students review the main ideas in this session by taking the quiz at the end of Lesson 3 in their Student Texts.

BALANCING A CHECKING ACCOUNT

Background:

In session three, students discovered that nearly half of all check writers don't use their checking accounts properly. They make many errors, can only guess at how much they have in their accounts, and are never able to balance their checkbook.

Because of this, they end up paying overdraft charges and develop a bad reputation with local merchants. Some are even arrested for writing checks if they have insufficient funds to cover them.

Avoiding these problems isn't hard, but consistency in balancing the checkbook is required. This lesson teaches how to perform this essential monthly chore.

Lesson Aim:
• To help the students use a checking account correctly and complete one full month of budget record keeping, plus a second month for essential practice (see "For Additional Study").

Advance Preparation

☐ Make one photocopy of Form 6, "Checking Account Reconciliation," for each student.

☐ Arrange the room so that students can work in groups during Getting Started and in pairs for Step 2.
  If you intend to assign a second month of record keeping as homework, have available:
  ☐ twelve more copies of Form 3, "Individual Account Sheet";
  ☐ ten more copies of Form 5, "Blank Checks";
  ☐ one more copy of Form 6, "Checking Account Reconciliation," for each student.

☐ Mount five large sheets of paper on the wall or bulletin board.

☐ On the top of each sheet write one of the following headings: "Deposits," "Allocated Funds," "Write Checks," "Record Expenses," "Balance."

☐ Provide two or three felt pens for each sheet.

GETTING STARTED (10 minutes)

Divide students into five groups and assign each group one of the five sheets. Instruct each group to work together to list in sequence the necessary steps for their assigned part of the budget process. What actions need to be taken to make and record deposits, allocate funds to various budget categories, write checks, and record and balance expenditures in the individual account sheets?

Point out that these are the basics of keeping a budget, and if the students do not understand them, they will be lost in future lessons. Allow four or five minutes for groups to work, then have a volunteer from each group share the steps they wrote down. Invite the rest of the class to suggest any needed modifications in the lists as they are presented.

STEP 1
Completing One Month of "Business"
(30 minutes)

Objective: To have the students correctly complete one full month of "business."

By the conclusion of the previous lesson, the students should have done the following:

☐ Filled out the heading on twelve individual account sheets—eleven categories and one checkbook ledger;

☐ Completed a deposit slip for their first paycheck and entered that amount in their checkbook ledger;

☐ Made "deposits" in each of their individual account sheet categories;

☐ Written one check each from categories 1, 3, 4, 8, and 9;

☐ Recorded these checks in their checkbook ledger and in the respective individual accounts and calculated their final balances.

1. Now have them continue the process. They will need to use their imaginations in writing checks. Instruct them to refer to the "Division of Pay" sheet, then write checks for all likely expenses in each category for the first half of the month. Have them make up logical dates, and create fictitious names for the companies or persons with whom they do business.

    Be sure to include all undesignated categories like food, clothing, entertainment, recreation and miscellaneous, making up realistic purchases in amounts that are within each category's budgeted amount.

2. When they have completed this for the first half of the month, they should make a second paycheck deposit for January 15 (1-15). Then they should proceed to fill out the remainder of the month in the same fashion they did the first half.

    For an example, look at the sample checkbook ledger in Lesson 3 (Step 2) of the Student Text.

    The only individual account sheet categories that can legitimately not show any expenditures are—

    1—Charitable Giving (if they chose to not give any away),

7 —Debts (since they shouldn't have any).

All other categories should list expenditures, the totals of which approach the budgeted monthly allotment.

STEP 2
Catching Errors Before They Catch You *(10 minutes)*

Objective: To have the students review each other's budget-keeping in an effort to catch errors.

1. Have the class divide into pairs. Instruct the partners to review each other's accounts by answering these questions:
  • Does the total of the balances of all the individual account sheets equal the balance at the end of the checkbook ledger?
  • Are there logical expenditures in each category where there should be transactions?
  • Has any category been overlooked?
  • Has any category exceeded its budgeted amount?
2. If there are errors or problems, have the students correct them as homework. They should follow the directions for Step 2 in the Student Text.

STEP 3
Calculating Check Service Fees *(10 minutes)*

Objective: To have the students calculate check service fees in their personal records.

1. Share the following:

In Lesson 6 we will evaluate the benefits of various checking account options—those accounts which offer free checking for preserving a minimum balance in your account versus those that charge a fee for each check.

However, for our present purposes, we will assume that your account charges a ten-cent fee for each check that you write.

Some checkbook ledgers provide a method for adding that fee to the amount of each check. However, it is easier to add a total amount at the end of the month . . . provided you never drain your account so low that the fees would put you into the red.

The way to calculate the fees at the end of the month is simply to count the number of checks you wrote that month. Then multiply the amount by ten cents (or whatever your per-check fee happens to be) and subtract that amount from the balance on your checkbook ledger.

2. Instruct the students to calculate and enter their check fees on their checkbook ledger. They should. . .

1. Use ten cents per check as the fee.
2. Write the date and the reason for the entry on the transaction part of the line.
3. Put the total amount in the withdrawal column.
4. Recalculate the balance.
5. Record this charge on the "Miscellaneous" individual account sheet. (It's an expense that needs to be accounted for just like any other.)

STEP 4
Reconciling Your Checkbook Ledger and Bank Statement (10 minutes)

Objective: To have the students practice reconciling their checkbook and "bank statement."

1. Distribute one copy of Form 6, "Checking Account Reconciliation," to each student. Explain that on a monthly basis the bank sends account statements to each of its customers. This statement records each deposit, withdrawal (checks they have processed), fees, and the balance for that account. The bank statement is essential for checking a person's financial record keeping.

2. Have each student follow the directions on Form 6 to come up with a simulated bank statement total. Each student's "bank balance" derived from Form 6 should be the same as the checkbook ledger balance. If the figures do not agree, there has been an error that needs to be found and corrected.

3. Explain that in real life the bank's statement will not include some of the most recent checks that have been written since they may not have been processed yet. Nor will it show any deposits made after the end of the bank's accounting period. Most bank statements have a work area and instructions for incorporating the unprocessed transactions along with the bank's balance. By following these steps, a new balance is produced which should agree with each person's personal ledger.

This Is Your Life

Applying what they've learned to their present finances. The following appears in the Student Text.

1. Home stretch! Keep that running list of income and outgo up to date!
2. If you have a checking account, be sure you keep a running balance by subtracting each check written from the total. When your monthly bank statement arrives, be sure to reconcile it with what your checkbook says.

FOR ADDITIONAL STUDY

Have any students whose budget didn't balance make the corrections as homework.

For additional study, have the students do the following (which appears in their Student Texts):

1. Why is it important to do double-entry record keeping? Find two people who keep budgets, at least one of whom uses some form of a double-entry system. Ask both of them whether they have ever made any errors. How did they find their errors? How long has it usually taken them to find their errors? What might have happened if they had not found them?
2. Carry over your balances from your ''January'' records and do a second month of budget keeping, following the second month of examples in Appendix E.

Be sure to provide all the additional copies of the required forms for each student. (See the Advance Preparation for the number of each.) It will probably take each student at least an hour to do another month of budget keeping.

LOANS AND CREDIT CARDS

Background:

When faced with a cash problem, many people pull out their credit cards. When more cash is needed, they may take out a loan. When their bills amount to more than their income, they resort to a "consolidation loan." This means that they take out a loan to cover all their other debts. However, the interest they pay on the consolidation loan usually exceeds what they would have paid on their initial debts, let alone what they would have paid in cash. . . if they would have had it.

If they are married, this financial burden will undoubtedly place heavy stress on the couple. Without knowing what is the root of their problems, they will blame each other. Financial problems account for nearly 90 percent of all divorces in America. Within two years both parties are likely to marry someone just like their first spouse, and the cycle will start all over.

Whether or not these people are married, many will go into bankruptcy.

All these tragedies can be avoided with a proper understanding of the dangers of living on borrowed money and how to use credit sparingly (if at all) and safely.

Advance Preparation:

☐ Prepare transparencies, Visual 4, "Steps in Budgeting," and Visual 5, "Installment Payments."

If you intend to assign a third month of record keeping as homework, have available for each student:

☐ twelve more copies of Form 3, "Individual Account Sheet";

☐ one more copy of Form 4, "Bank Deposits";

☐ ten more copies of Form 5, "Blank Checks";

☐ and one more copy of Form 6, "Checking Account Reconciliation."

☐ If you have not already scheduled a banker as a resource person for next week's lesson and wish to have such a guest speaker, do so now. See Step 3 in Lesson 6 for further details on how you should use this resource person.

Getting Started (15 minutes)

At this point in the course each student should have—

☐ at least one month's income and expenses budgeted (two months if they did the "For Additional Study" section),

☐ all bills paid for that month, and

☐ money reserved for the irregular expenses that come up less often than once a month.

Lesson Aim:
- **To help the students understand how interest rates are calculated.**
- **To warn them of the dangers of living on borrowed money.**
- **To give them some advice on how to use credit safely.**
- **To help students maintain their budgets for a third month. (See "For Additional Study.")**

Display Visual 4, "Steps in Budgeting," to review the process that the class has gone through so far.

- If the students' budgets, individual account sheets, checkbook ledgers, and bank statements all balance, they are doing great.
- If they do not, they need to go back and work on them until they do.
- If any students are having problems, refer them to the Getting Started section of Lesson 5 in the Student Text for a more complete review of the steps. You may need to arrange to give them special help in resolving their problems.
- If you assigned a second month of budget keeping last lesson and have time, encourage the students to divide into pairs and go over each other's records. Circulate through the class, assisting where problems are encountered.

If your budgets don't balance but you have not made any errors in arithmetic, then the problem may be that you are spending more than you are earning. This is an all-too-common problem and causes people more problems than they realize.

This brings us to the subject of this lesson: loans.

Ask: "Why do many people take out a loan? What are some of the advantages/disadvantages of borrowing money?"

Be prepared to share some of these problems which result from exceeding budget expenses:

When bills amount to more than the income, people may resort to a "consolidation loan." This means that they take out a loan to cover all their other debts. However, the consolidation loan is often only a "stopgap" measure unless they also change their spending patterns. In any case, the cost of borrowing is always much more than what they would have paid in cash—if they had saved for it.

STEP 1
Understanding Interest Rates (10 minutes)

Objective: To help students understand how interest rates are calculated, and the real "cost" of using borrowed money.

1. Ask, "What does the word 'interest' mean when we're talking about borrowing money?" Be prepared to expand on your students' answers if need be by pointing out that when you borrow money, the lender expects to make a profit. It's his or her money, and you are just "renting it." The way the lender

"collects rent" is by charging interest, the fee for using another person's money.

2. Explain the way simple interest is calculated:

> A simple interest loan means that the interest you pay is calculated each month on the unpaid balance. For example, let's assume you borrowed $1,000 at 12 percent annual interest to be paid back in ten monthly installments. The 12 percent annual interest is the same as 1 percent interest per month. Therefore, the payments would be calculated approximately as is shown in Visual 5, "Installment Payments."

Display Visual 5 and point out how the payments are calculated.

> In reality, the actual figures do not break down so neatly in even dollar amounts. The total payments, including interest, would be added together and then divided by ten so that each monthly payment would be equal—in this case $105.58 per month. Point out that the total amount of interest would be $55.80.

3. Explain the way add-on interest is calculated:

> Several years ago a law was passed by the United States Congress called "The Truth in Lending Act." It requires that all interest be stated by its APR (Annualized Percentage Rate). This means how it would compare with a "simple" interest loan.
>
> Add-on interest is calculated over the length of the loan and not on the unpaid balance each month. Thus the total interest paid is significantly higher. Also, the payment schedule is designed so that most of the interest is paid up-front; thus there is little savings in paying the loan off early. In addition, whether the loan is fixed or variable can make a big difference in how much you ultimately pay.

4. Summarize this section on the cost of borrowing:

> The actual cost is seen to be even higher when compared with saving for an expenditure. Not only must the borrower pay interest, but any interest which would be earned from savings is lost, often doubling the real cost of the loan!

STEP 2
The Dangers of Living on Borrowed Money
(15 minutes)

Objective: Describe the risks of living on borrowed money.

Because it has become increasingly popular in our society to live on borrowed money, it is important for the students to understand the risks and disadvantages of doing this. Review the following, writing the figures and main points on the chalkboard.

A. **It is expensive.** The money paid in interest can always be used better for other purposes.

> Let's suppose you took out a $1,000 loan at 15 percent interest to buy a new living room set. You arrange to pay it back over a three-year period at about $35 per month. Your costs would look like this:

The store price of the purchase	$1,000
The amount of interest over three years	248
TOTAL OUTLAY	$1,248

> Ask, "What are some better things you could do with $248?"
>
> List ideas on the chalkboard.
>
> Then ask, "What does this insight tell you about only considering the amount of the monthly payment?" (Even when a payment plan can be handled, the interest fee reduces the buyer's ability to use money for other purposes.)

B. **It is addictive.** Money needed to pay for past debts cannot be used to meet current needs.

> Not only do you lose your freedom of choice, but you are tempted to borrow more money as the only seeming solution when you encounter unforeseen expenses. Let's say your car breaks down and the repair costs $150. You may feel forced to borrow again. Whereas, if you had been saving for that living room set instead of paying for it on time, you would at least have the choice of using some of that money for the car repair and postponing the furniture.

> Display Visual 1, "Suggested Percentages." Ask, "What will happen to the other areas of your budget if debt grows?" After students respond, point out that this situation will be explored more fully in Lesson 6.

C. **It is deceptive.** Ask, "Why do you think merchants are willing to go through all the paperwork of credit card sales plus

pay the credit card company a percentage of every sale?"
(Research has shown that people will spend as much as 20
percent more when shopping on credit as when shopping with
cash. Somehow it is easier to buy now and pay later.
Apparently, when people have to put down their cold, hard
cash on the spot in order to make a purchase, they are more
careful.)

Most of us need to be more conservative shoppers.

STEP 3
Tips for Using Credit or Borrowing Money
(20 minutes)

Objective: To help the students evaluate tips on the wise use of
credit and particularly credit cards.

Lead a class discussion of the following tips for using credit or
borrowing money. Have the students take turns reading the tips
as they appear under Step 3 of the Student Text. Then invite
discussion of each point. Ask questions such as:

"Why is this point important?"

"What examples have you seen which prove this point's value?"

"What might be conditions under which this point would not
apply?"

1. **Never borrow money needlessly.** For instance, never
   borrow money to purchase an ego trip. Never borrow for
   an impulse purchase. Wait to consider it.

2. **Remember that you will always have to pay for what
   you borrow.** Even if you should go bankrupt, you'll pay
   in years of bad reputation, no credit, inconvenience, and
   other painful losses.

3. **Weigh the pros and cons.** Make certain that the
   benefits of borrowing far exceed the cost of the loan
   liability and the restrictions the burden of repayment
   will put on your future.

4. **Make certain that your purchase will last longer
   than it takes to pay for it.** It is a good goal never to purchase a depreciable (declining in value) item on credit—
   i.e., a car or appliance.

5. **Set a goal to use your credit cards only if you can pay
   off the entire amount by the due date.** Credit card interest is terribly high. *If you can't control your credit
   card use, destroy them.*

6. **If you experience a problem making payments, go**

immediately to your creditor. Explain the situation and work out an agreeable arrangement. Do everything you can to save your credit rating.

7. **Never loan out your credit cards to anyone you wouldn't allow free access to your cash.** If a credit card is lost or stolen, report it immediately to limit your liability.

This Is Your Life

Applying what they've learned to their present finances. The following appears in the student book.

1. Congratulations on keeping track of your money for a whole month! Use this record to do the following:

    a. Total up your income; total your expenditures (plus any money you have left over). How do the actual totals compare to your estimated monthly income and estimated Net Spendable Income?

    b. Now list each of your expenditures from the past month under one of the categories you created on the "Individual Account Sheets" (Form 3). (For example: List the $3.40 for pizza and $5.39 at McDonald's under the Food category. List the $9.80 you spent for gas under Transportation; etc.) Add up the expenses in each category; figure what percentage each total is of your NSI. How do your actual amounts and percentages for each category compare to the estimated budget you figured out earlier? (See "This Is Your Life," Lesson 3, #3.)

    c. Do you like what you see? Were your earlier estimated percentages and amounts realistic? Is too much going for pizza and bowling and not enough for clothes? Using the record of your actual income and expenses for one month, make a budget for next month. What percentage of your NSI do you want to allot to each category? Calculate what that percentage would be in actual dollars.

    d. Using the budget you have just created, begin keeping a record of actual income and expenses once again. This time, however, record each expenditure under its proper category and deduct it from the amount you have budgeted for it this month. Try to remain within the amounts allotted.

2. Have you recently borrowed money from your parents? a friend? the bank? How are you paying it back—a portion each month? in one lump sum? Are you paying interest? If so, figure how much you will pay altogether. Do you have to borrow money often? Can you think of another way to plan for those expenses?

FOR ADDITIONAL STUDY

To review the main ideas of this topic, assign the students to take the quiz at the end of Lesson 5 in their Student Texts.

Instruct students to read the two brief articles in their Student books: ''One Big Borrowing Decision'' (dealing with paying for college) and ''Savings and Investments: Keys to Avoiding Debt.''

Assign a third month of budget keeping, following the third month of examples in Appendix E. Be sure to provide all the additional copies of the required forms for each student. (See the Advance Preparation for the number of each.) It will probably take each student at least an hour to do another month of budget keeping, but it is time well-spent!

COPING WITH BUDGET BUSTERS

Background:

Everyone encounters unexpected expenses from time to time. Since a good budget accounts for where all money goes—even that which you saved or designated as miscellaneous—there may not be enough funds for the unexpected expense. It can become a "budget buster" unless the budget can bend.

A person who does not know how to adjust the budget is likely to abandon the budget as an unhelpful tool.

This lesson teaches ways to meet unforeseen expenses by anticipating some and adjusting for the truly unforeseeable.

Advance Preparation:

☐ Check that the banker you have invited will be coming for the last part of this lesson. Confirm time and directions. Go over the content of Step 3 to provide suggestions of what would be the most helpful outside input.

☐ For this lesson have ready one copy for each student of Form 1, "Monthly Income and Expenses" and Form 7, the "Loan Application," from the Student Text.

    If you intend to assign a fourth month of record keeping as homework, have available for each student:

    ☐ twelve more copies of Form 3, "Individual Account Sheet";

    ☐ ten more copies of Form 5, "Blank Checks";

    ☐ one more copy of Form 6, "Checking Account Reconciliation."

☐ If you have not already scheduled a life insurance agent for next week's lesson and wish to have such a guest speaker, do so now. See Steps 2 and 3 in Lesson 7 for further details on how you should use this resource person.

Getting Started (5 minutes)

It would be great if budgeting in real life were merely a matter of keeping track of one's income and planned expenses each month. Unfortunately, unplanned expenses do occur, and they must be paid.

Describe an unplanned expense that you recently encountered, a real "budget buster" that you did not anticipate.

If you cannot think of any, use the following:

    The Johnsons were returning from an out-of-state visit with relatives. Darkness was coming on, and it had begun to snow when they got off the expressway for something to eat.

Lesson Aim:

• **To help students understand how a budget can adjust to meet unexpected expenses.**

• **To evaluate several checking account options offered by most banks.**

• **To help students maintain a fourth month of budgeting (See "For Additional Study").**

Suddenly, as they pulled away from a stoplight, their car's "charge" warning light came on. They checked the most simple causes—a broken belt or a burned fuse. A fuse was indeed burned, but replacing it didn't solve the problem. The real source was more serious.

It was too late for a garage to be open. On such a dark, snowy night, it would have been foolish to continue driving if the real problem was a blown alternator. With headlights, windshield wipers, and heater going, the battery wouldn't have lasted more than ten miles.

So they got a room in a motel. The next morning a nearby garage confirmed that the alternator needed replacing. Repairs, the motel, and extra restaurant meals for the family came to $260—expenses they could not have prevented or predicted.

It was an anxious eighteen hours before they got everything fixed and arrived safely home. Their credit card covered the immediate expenses, but would they be able to pay the full credit card bill three weeks later? How could they find out?

Invite students to suggest how the Johnsons could find out if they could pay the bill.

Then introduce this week's challenge:

This week you will each face a "budget buster"—an unexpected expense. This problem will show that budgeting is a dynamic process. Your budget is not a straitjacket, but a tool to help you manage your money. Therefore, when unexpected variables arise, your budget needs to change to meet the need.

STEP 1
A "Budget Buster" (15 minutes)

Objective: To guide each student through the process of meeting an unexpected expense.

1. Guide the group through the example below (also in the Student book) which shows how someone might handle a "budget buster."

Suppose you have a $30,000 per year income and have completed one month of record keeping. Your budget buster is an auto accident for which you were at fault. You have a fine of $35 to pay and car repairs of $1,500. Your insurance has a $100 deductible. Let's also suppose that you have $45.40 remaining in your auto account but only $31.40 of that can be used for repairs. The rest must be saved for license and insurance later in the year.

Both the fine and the deductible must be worked into your budget. (It's times like this when you are glad to have paid that costly insurance premium.)

2. Have the students turn to the example under Step 1 in their Student Texts to see how the traffic fine was paid out of Category 12, "Miscellaneous." The deductible amount for the repairs ($100) was paid out of Category 5, "Auto" ($31.40 that was already there plus a transfer of $68.60 from Category 10, "Savings"). In this case, there was enough surplus in savings to cover the expense, so a loan was unnecessary.

3. Have the students turn to Appendix C, "Budget Busters," in the back of their Student books. There they will find their personal budget buster according to their income level and the number of months of budgeting they have completed.

A. If your annual income is below $25,500, and you have completed one or two months of record keeping: You just broke your glasses and had to have them replaced for $118. Your insurance does not cover this unexpected medical bill.

B. If your income is above $25,500, and you have completed one or two months of record keeping: You had an automobile accident where you were at fault. You received a $35 fine and did $1,500 worth of damage to your car. Fortunately, your insurance will cover the repairs except for the $100 deductible. The total cost of the accident to you is $135.

C. If your income is below $25,500, but you have completed three months of budgeting: A close relative has just died and you had to go to the funeral—$210 for the trip.

D. If your income is above $25,500, but you have completed three months of budgeting: You just received notice that you underpaid your income taxes last year and you owe $2,100 additional taxes and fees. The IRS will finance the debt for a minimum payment of $250.00 and monthly payments of $100 at 18 percent (APR) interest over the next twenty-two months. (This will require you to fill out a new Form 1, "Monthly Income and Expenses," to include the repayment of debt.)

Besides these options, if you have any "attorneys" or "doctors" in your class, make these changes for them:

- Attorneys: double either option "B" or "D" (depending on how many months of budget keeping have been completed).

- Doctors: triple either option "B" or "D."

The students' responsibility is to adjust their budgets to cover this expense. The adjustments should be added as transactions on the end of the last month they have completed. To do this they may need to dip into their savings.

STEP 2
Taking Out a Loan (20 minutes)

Objective: To have students practice applying for a loan and then adjusting their budgets to accommodate their debt.

Those whose expenses exceed what can be covered by the appropriate category, plus their savings, must take out a loan. Its repayment must be incorporated into their budget for future months (if you are assigning the "For Additional Study").

Those who do not need a loan should go through this step anyway for educational purposes. Instruct them to apply for a loan equal to one month's NSI. However, when they have completed the exercise, they do not need to incorporate the repayment of the loan into their future budget. They may continue using their established budget.

Have the students look at Step 2 in the Student Text and follow the directions for securing a loan.

STEP 3
Evaluating Checking Account Options (20 minutes)

Objective: To introduce students to the advantages and disadvantages of three checking account options.

1. Invite the guest speaker, a banker, to explain the basic checking account options his or her bank offers, focusing on the following content. Or, if you have not engaged an outside speaker, share the following information with the class.

   There are many options available for checking accounts, but we will focus on three common options and their advantages and disadvantages:

   Minimum deposit checking. Most banks, savings and loans, etc., offer no-fee checking for customers who maintain an average minimum balance in their accounts, usually $500 or more. Otherwise one has to pay a fee for each check written, plus a minimum service charge per month.

In evaluating whether or not to leave a portion of your savings in a checking account that pays no interest so that you can maintain your balance above the no-fee minimum, consider the cost versus the earnings.

For example: if a bank offered free checking with a minimum deposit of $500, or would pay you 6 percent interest (APR) on the money in savings, it might seem better to leave the money in savings. However, if you're charged ten cents per check, plus a monthly service charge of $3.00 and you write thirty checks per month, that's $6.00 per month for checking. You would have to earn over 14 percent (APR) on your $500 to match the cost of checking. You're much better off financially to take advantage of their minimum deposit/free checking offer.

Automatic tellers. Most banks offer automatic tellers for banking transactions after regular business hours. These can be a great convenience, but they can also be easily misused.

The most common problem associated with automatic tellers is withdrawing cash and not recording it in the checkbook ledger. This error gives the impression of more money in checking than is really there, often resulting in overdrawn accounts. To avoid problems:

First, keep withdrawals within your budget. If you take cash out because you have spent all your budgeted cash, you're robbing money that you'll need for something else later.

Second, record all withdrawals whether they are made by check, automatic teller, cashier, etc. When you use an automatic teller, make a regular habit of recording it as soon as you get home.

Third, know if your bank assesses a fee for the use of the automatic teller. Calculate this cost into any transaction.

Automatic overdraft protection. Many banks offer a service that will pay overdrawn checks rather than return them because of insufficient funds. This sounds great on the surface, but it leads to some very sad consequences.

Because they know overdrawn checks are going to be paid, many people are tempted to overdraw their accounts regularly.

Also, this feature encourages those who don't like to balance their checkbook ledgers to be slothful and not do

FOR ADDITIONAL STUDY

Instruct students to review this topic by taking the quiz at the end of Lesson 6 in their Student Texts.

Assign a fourth month of budget keeping, incorporating the results of this lesson's budget buster (simply depleting reserves or requiring a loan). Have students refer to the fourth month of examples in Appendix E. Be sure to provide all the additional copies of the required forms for each student. (See the Advance Preparation for the number of each.) It will probably take each student at least an hour to do another month of budget keeping.

so because they feel it is not necessary.

Finally, overdrafts are charged to the customer's credit card account, and interest is charged just as if the credit card had been used to obtain cash. Cash drawn on credit cards begins accumulating interest charges immediately and at the credit card's very high rate. This can lead to a lot of debt in a hurry.

At best, an automatic overdraft system encourages bad habits. At worst, it can lead to unmanageable debt. Remember, when you reach the debt limit, the bank will no longer honor the overdraft protection, so you'll be right back where you started, only deeply in debt as well. So it's better never to start using the overdraft protection in the first place.

2. Lead a time of question and answers about general banking services and particularly the various checking account options.

This Is Your Life

Applying what they've learned to their present finances. The following appears in the Student Text.

1. Continue to record your expenditures on the "Individual Account Sheets" by category. Deduct from the amount you have allotted for each category as you go, so you can see at a glance what you have left to spend.

2. Think back: What unplanned expense (a real-life Budget Buster!) have you had to cope with in the last four months? (Dent in the car fender? Big date that cost more than you planned?) How did you cope with it: did your parents bail you out? have savings to cover? borrow and pay back?

3. Think ahead: Does your current budget allow some leeway for future unplanned expenses?

4. If you have a checking account, what checking account options are you using—free checking for minimum deposit? automatic teller privilege? overdraft protection? Have they helped or hindered you in "living within your means"?

UNDERSTANDING INSURANCE

Background:

The purpose of life insurance is to provide financially for a loved one should the policy holder die. Unfortunately, life insurance is sometimes billed as a way to enable survivors to prosper or as an ideal savings plan.

A policy set up to enable the survivors to prosper creates the rather ominous situation of the loved one being better off financially with the policy holder dead. Who wants that kind of arrangement?

A life insurance policy may be a better savings plan than nothing. It has a strong appeal for the person who isn't disciplined enough to save in any other way. However, there aren't many other advantages. Much better rates can be found elsewhere.

This lesson will help the students understand the purpose of life insurance and how to determine the appropriate amount and type for differing needs.

Advance Preparation:

☐ Check that the life insurance agent you invited will be coming for this lesson as your guest speaker. Confirm time and directions, etc. Go over the content of Steps 2 and 3 to provide suggestions of what would be the most helpful outside input.

☐ Prepare transparencies, Visual 6, "Evaluating Life Insurance," and Visual 7, "Comparing Term and Whole Life Insurance."

☐ Have available for each student one copy of Form 8, "Insurance Needs Worksheet."

If you intend to assign a fifth month of record keeping as homework, have available for each student:

☐ twelve more copies of Form 3, "Individual Account Sheet";

☐ one more copy of Form 4, "Bank Deposits";

☐ ten more copies of Form 5, "Blank Checks";

☐ one more copy of Form 6, "Checking Account Reconciliation."

Lesson Aim:

- To help the students understand the purpose and value of life insurance.
- To help them understand how their needs for life insurance can be calculated and the types of insurance that are available.
- To help students maintain their budgets for a fifth month (See "For Additional Study.")

Getting Started (10 minutes)

Have students work in groups of three to review how they incorporated the budget buster from the previous lesson into their budgets. The adjustments should have been added as transactions on the end of the last month they completed before Lesson 6. For those who have gone on to do a fourth month of budgeting, the consequences of the budget buster should have been carried over into that month.

Instruct students to compare the impact of the unexpected

expense on their budget. "How were you able to pay that expense?" "What difference will that expense make on your next month's budget?"

STEP 1
Evaluating Life Insurance (10 minutes)

Objective: To prepare students to evaluate life insurance in terms of the amount needed and what is affordable.

1. Explain that the purpose of life insurance is to provide for a loved one after you die. Most young people don't concern themselves with selecting life insurance at this age, but eventually they will, especially as they assume responsibility and commitments for a family.

2. Point out that there are three basic questions each person must consider about life insurance:
   - How much do I need?
   - How much can I afford?
   - What kind is best?

   Use the illustration in the Student Text as an example of how to answer these questions. On the overhead projector, display Visual 6, "Evaluating Life Insurance." Insert a sheet of paper under the transparency to cover everything but the first question. As you present the details of the illustration, lower the mask to disclose the facts.

   Imagine a young family of four where the husband is the primary wage earner, making $24,000 a year.

   How much insurance do they need?

   The wage earner makes $24,000 per year. Social Security survivors' benefits would pay roughly $11,000 per year to his wife and children, leaving a deficit of $13,000 per year. Therefore, the death benefits (the money paid to the beneficiaries of the insurance policy) would need to be large enough so that when it was invested at—let's say—10 percent interest, it would yield $13,000 per year. Since $13,000 is 10 percent of $130,000, that is the size of policy that would be needed ($13,000/year 10% = $130,000).

   So now we know the answer to the first question: The husband should take out $130,000 worth of life insurance.

   How much can they afford?

   This can be answered by referring to the insurance category of their budget on Form 1, "Monthly Income and Expenses." Let's assume that the maximum amount they can afford is $15 of their NSI (net spendable income) per month.

3. Make a transition from this presentation into Step 2 by pointing out that the answer to the third question (What kind is best for them?) is determined by their need for a $130,000 policy and their available funds (a maximum of $15 per month). Step 2 deals with the types of insurance.

STEP 2
Types of Insurance (25 minutes)

Objective: To prepare students to evaluate the basic types of life insurance.

1. Instruct half the class to read the Student Text information on "Term insurance." Direct the other half to read about "Whole-Life insurance." Tell them that they will be asked to report to the class on the type of insurance you have assigned to them. Allow two or three minutes for them to read.

2. Ask, "What did you find out about *term* insurance?" (It is initially the least expensive and is the only choice when funds are severely limited. Term insurance means that it is purchased for a set period of time, i.e., one year, five years, ten years, etc.. At the end of each period the policy can be renewed, but the cost goes up and generally will continue to do so as long as you own it. (It goes up with increasing age because the potential for death and therefore a claim on the policy increases.)

3. Ask, "What did you find out about *whole-life* insurance?" (Whole-life insurance means that it is purchased for the insured's lifetime—that's why it's called "whole-life." Whole-life insurance is initially more expensive than term, but it accumulates a cash reserve that can be used to offset payments at a later time. In most whole-life policies—also called cash-value policies, the cash reserves belong to the insurance company. The reserve is set aside to offset the increasing age of the insured. The policyholder can borrow against the cash value, but it becomes a debt—plus interest— against the payout if the insured dies. It usually has a monthly or yearly fee that starts out higher than a term policy, but is not increased with age. If the insurance company also pays dividends—earnings—to the policyholder, the dividends belong to the policy owner and can be used to offset the policy's cost or to purchase more insurance.)

4. Display Visual 7, "Comparing Term and Whole-Life

Insurance." Then explain that the transparency illustration of term and whole-life insurance compares how they work.

5. Point out that since term insurance is always cheaper initially, it usually represents the best alternative for anyone with limited funds. In our example, this husband would have to buy term insurance because of the need for a $130,000 policy and only $15 a month available to pay the premiums.

6. Mention that there is a third type of life insurance, and that is a "paid-up" policy. For this you invest a one-time, large sum of money to purchase coverage.

7. Introduce your guest speaker, the life insurance agent, explaining that he or she will share the basic policies available. While many companies offer numerous small variations to the basic options, the speaker will keep this presentation simple.

8. If your guest does not explain the following items, raise these questions (and any others you feel will be of interest to your class):
   - What are actuarial or mortality tables and how are they figured?
   - Does your company offer special rates to nonsmokers or for health programs?
   - Which occupations (such as pilots) or activities (such as scuba diving) would increase the rates?
   - What benefits are possible through group plans?

STEP 3
Selecting Life Insurance (15 minutes)

Objective: To help the students practice calculating how much insurance they would need.

1. Distribute a copy of Form 8, "Insurance Needs Worksheet," to each student. Explain that they are to calculate how much insurance they would need. Give the following instructions:
   - Assume that you are the sole source of income for your household and that Social Security would provide $11,000 per year should you die.
   - On the form, Line 3 equals your family's additional annual need.
   - Line 4 is found by multiplying Line 3 by ten because we are assuming the life insurance settlement could be invested at 10 percent interest, which could be drawn on annually.
   - To determine the lump-sum costs, include the total amount of any debt you have included, $3,000 for

funeral costs, and $40,000 for the college education of each child. Calculate for two children.

2. Once the students have finished their calculations, ask different ones to volunteer the amount of life insurance that they would need.

3. Then ask the guest speaker to estimate the monthly cost of the various amounts of insurance the students would need. Have him or her quote both term and whole-life costs. Make sure the class understands that these are only "ballpark" estimates to give the students an idea of the cost of life insurance.

This Is Your Life

Applying what they've learned to their present finances. The following appears in the student book.

1. Two weeks of spending by your budget—how's it going? Have you overspent in one category and had to borrow from another? Just be sure to keep track of all expenses.

2. What kind of insurance—if any—do you need at this point in your life: auto; driver's; student; sports medical? Who is paying for it? What are the benefits? What is the monthly premium? If you don't know—find out!

FOR ADDITIONAL STUDY

Instruct the students to review this session by taking the quiz at the end of Lesson 7 in their Student books.

Assign a fifth month of budget keeping, following the examples in Appendix E. Be sure to provide all the additional copies of the required forms for each student. (See the Advance Preparation for the number of each.)

BUYING CARS

Background:

The auto industry is big business. It stays big partially through effective sales techniques that attempt to convince people to buy a more expensive car than they can afford—usually by buying on credit.

Automobiles are one of the largest purchases most people make, and they are usually the first large purchase for young people. Getting strapped by excessive auto payments is often one of the first major financial mistakes of youth.

Young people need to determine what kind of transportation they really need. Then learning how to shop for the best deal in obtaining that transportation can save much grief.

Advance Preparation:

☐ Gather enough copies of the automotive section of a local newspaper for each pair of students to have a copy. (They don't all have to be current.)

☐ Borrow and have available as many copies as possible of a consumer products rating service such as *Consumer Reports* magazine's "Annual Auto Issue" or the "Buying Guide." (Attempt to have one for every four students. They do not need to be current.)

☐ From an insurance agent, secure a supply of rating sheets showing typical insurance costs of recent-model popular cars.

☐ Make one copy for each student of Form 9, the "Car Selection Worksheet."

   If you intend to assign a sixth month of record keeping as homework, have available for each student:

   ☐ twelve more copies of Form 3, "Individual Account Sheet";
   ☐ ten more copies of Form 5, "Blank Checks";
   ☐ one more copy of Form 6, "Checking Account Reconciliation."

☐ If you have not already scheduled a real estate agent for next week's lesson and wish to have such a guest speaker, do so now. See the Getting Started section in Lesson 10 for further details on how you should use this resource person.

Getting Started (10 minutes)

Ask students the following questions and write their responses on the chalkboard.

- How many of you drive the family car?
- How many of you contribute to the expenses of that car?
- How many of you own a car of your own?
- How many of you are making payments on your car?

Lesson Aim:
- **To help students understand the variables in shopping for a car.**
- **To give them the opportunity to simulate the basic research for selecting a car to buy.**
- **To help students maintain their budgeting for a sixth and final month. (See "For Additional Study.")**

(If your students are open enough with each other, ask what the payments are. Then calculate the average payment among those who are making payments.)

- How many of you hope to buy a car within the next year?

Share the following:

As you can see, purchasing a car is something many of us have already faced or will soon face. We're a mobile society, and even within large cities with public transportation systems, most people own cars.

The two largest purchases most people will make with their personal finances are houses and cars. It is important to know how and where to get the best deals. In this study, we'll concentrate on cars.

Ask, "Besides providing transportation, what else do cars represent?" (For many people, a car expresses the image of who they think they are or would like to be. Therefore, they are prone to spend too much.)

Explain that this lesson will look at four decision areas:

- buying new cars,
- leasing cars,
- buying used cars, and
- financing.

STEP 1
Buying a New Car (5 minutes)

Objective: To identify the pros and cons for buying a new car.

1. Ask, "What are some of the pluses of buying a new car?" Student answers should touch on items such as:
   - There are few purchases more exciting than buying a new car, and an old car never seems so bad as when you begin looking at new ones.
   - You can sometimes get a lower interest rate on a new car loan than for a used car if you need to finance the purchase.
      The new car buyer does not have to worry about the car having been misused by a previous owner.
   - The manufacturer offers a warranty, promising to fix certain problems which may occur within a set time period or number of miles the car is driven.
2. Ask, "What are some of the minuses of buying a new car?" Student answers should touch on:
   - Most budgets cannot handle the cost of a new car.

- A common technique used in selling new cars is to de-emphasize the total cost and focus only on the monthly payments. These are often calculated based on the cheapest model over four to six years and may contain a "balloon" note as the last payment, which can range from several hundred to thousands of dollars.
- The depreciation (decline in value) on a new car is often as much as 25 percent of the purchase price as soon as the buyer signs the title papers. For example, the resale value of a new car financed at 80 percent of the purchase price over forty-eight months may not equal the amount owed until the last few months of the loan. Many new car buyers experience the shock of trying to sell a car, only to discover they owe several thousand dollars more than it's worth.
- Insurance costs are significantly higher on a new car.

STEP 2
Leasing a Car (5 minutes)

Objective: To identify the real costs of leasing a car.

Go over the chart in Step 2 of the Student Text to show the expense of leasing a car. Be sure to point out that few people who have the cash to buy a car outright would choose to lease it. Therefore, the "net opportunity cost" is only theoretical. The students should never allow a sales person to entice them by those nonexistent benefits.

STEP 3
Buying a Used Car (30 minutes)

Objective: To guide the students in simulating the basic research for selecting a car to buy.

1. Ask, "Why do many people hesitate to buy a used car?" Answers might include:
   - fear of getting stuck with someone else's problem,
   - desire to have the latest features,
   - desire for the prestige of a new car.
2. Respond to the answers students suggest. For example,
   Most used cars less than three years old are traded in because the owners got tired of them or they had relatively minor problems. That is not to say one can't get stuck with a defective car. It is possible...just as it is possible to get stuck with a defective new car. But a little knowledge and caution can virtually eliminate that risk.

3. Divide the class into pairs to work together to complete Form 9, the "Car Selection Worksheet." To each pair give:
   - Two copies of Form 9;
   - One copy of a local newspaper automotive/classified section.

Distribute around the class:
   - Copies of a consumer products rating service such as *Consumer Reports* magazine's "Annual Auto Issue" and their "Buying Guide;"
   - Sheets listing insurance costs for popular late-model cars. If you are unable to provide these, have the students skip the fifth step on the Car Selection Worksheet.

   Encourage the students to interact with their partners as they search for a car within the limitations of their simulated career and finances. Emphasize that insurance costs are often one of the major considerations in choosing a car. (Usually a young person can save money if his or her parents are the registered owners of the car and list it on their insurance policy. Also, the young person's driving record and academic status are important factors in setting insurance rates.)

STEP 4
Financing a Car (10 minutes)

Objective: To introduce students to some options for financing a car, then to have them simulate calculations for the cost of financing a car.

1. Reconvene the class and poll the amount that students intend to finance. Ask, "How surprised were you at the cost of cars you found? What was your response to how much (or little) you could spend?"
2. Ask, "How would the total cost and the monthly payments vary if you made a larger down payment?"
3. Share the following tips for financing a car when one must resort to that method.

   Low-interest loans. From time to time, car manufacturers will offer low-interest loans on new cars. However, there's an old cliché that says, "There are no free lunches." If you're offered a low-interest loan, there is a reason. Usually you will pay a higher price for the car than you would if you arranged your own financing and dealt with the dealer on a cash-purchase basis. Sometimes only certain models (usually the most expensive and fully equipped) qualify for the low-interest loan. In the end, you pay more than you intended.

Dealer-arranged financing. Many dealers will offer to arrange financing for you. This often complicates the sale and makes the actual sales price difficult to determine. Also, you may be able to get a lower interest rate by checking with several lenders (banks) of your own choosing or possibly the credit union at your work.

Collateral substitute. Because cars depreciate so rapidly, many lenders consider them a high-risk loan. Therefore, they carry a high interest rate. If you can provide alternative collateral for the loan, such as stocks, bonds, real estate, etc., you can usually reduce the interest rate on the loan. If you don't have other collateral, perhaps a parent or relative does, and would be willing to use it. Warning! If the loan is not repaid, the substitute collateral can be lost.

Co-signer. A young person can often get a better rate by having a parent co-sign on the loan. This means the parent accepts responsibility to pay off the loan if the young person is not able to do so. While this may look like a logical option, both parties need to honestly confront the implications of such an arrangement if something goes wrong.

4. Summarize this lesson by stressing that their future goal should be to be totally debt free, especially for depreciating items such as cars. Offer these three pieces of wise advice:
   - Buy a car within your budget.
   - Drive it until it is totally paid for.
   - Then save to buy the next one.

This Is Your Life

Applying what they've learned to their present finances. The following appears in the Student Text.

1. You should now have a record of your monthly expenses by category. Were you able to stay within the budgeted amounts for each category? If not, do you need to adjust the amount you have budgeted for each category—or simply work harder to stay within your budget?
2. Go on, that wasn't so bad. Why not fill out some new copies of the "Individual Account Sheets" (Form 3) for your personal budget categories? Then keep running records of your income and expenditures for the next month.
3. If you own your own car, are you making monthly payments?

52

Have the students take the quiz at the end of Lesson 9 in their Student books.

Assign a sixth month of budget keeping, following the examples in Appendix E. Be sure to provide all the additional copies of the required forms for each student. (See the Advance Preparation for the number of each.)

How much are you spending each month (including gas and maintenance) on transportation? Based on what you learned in this lesson, are you getting the most for your money?

4. If you don't own a car, but use your parents' car, what do you contribute toward car expenses? Is this expense part of your budget?

5. Do you use public transportation? What percent of your NSI goes toward transportation? Weighing owning a car versus public transportation, which is most workable and affordable for you now?

BUYING A FIRST HOME

Background:

Financially, there are few decisions more exciting—and foreboding—than selecting and buying a home. The young person who does not understand the options may be either too intimidated to try to buy a home, or may make a rash and financially unwise selection.

What is a reasonable percentage of one's income to spend on housing? What are the sources of financing and types of mortgages? What are the hidden costs in buying a house?

Some real estate agents and mortgage companies will allow a buyer to overextend just to close a deal. They are not much more protective of the client than the credit card companies.

This lesson attempts to provide an informative and helpful overview.

Advance Preparation:

☐ Check that the real estate agent you invited will be coming for this lesson as your guest speaker. Confirm time and directions, etc. Give the speaker a photocopy of Lesson 10 from this Teacher's Guide to outline the range of material (Steps 1-4) he or she should cover. Read the Getting Started section and decide together how you plan to lead the class.

☐ Make one copy for each student of Form 10, "What Home Can You Buy?" from the Student Text.

☐ Prepare a transparency for Visual 8, the "Adjustable Rate Mortgage," to display on the overhead projector.

☐ Secure several copies of the real estate section of a local newspaper. They do not all have to be from the same date.

☐ Write on the chalkboard or a blank overhead transparency: "Do you agree or disagree. . .? 'Owning your own home is a valid goal for everyone.'"

Lesson Aim:
• **To give the students a realistic and informative picture of what it is like to buy a first home.**

Getting Started (5 minutes)

Introduce this lesson by inviting responses to the agree/disagree statement. Ask students to express their reasons for agreement or disagreement. Then respond to their comments:

> This session will help you recognize some of the benefits and problems of home ownership. Buying a home is not just a matter of choosing the house you like and moving in. Only a limited amount of your budget can go to housing and that amount must cover the mortgage payments, taxes, utilities, etc. Now that you understand how to budget your monthly

income, you have a definite advantage over most young people.

Buying a home involves much more than just paying the mortgage each month. First, it is necessary to save enough money for your down payment (usually 10—20 percent of the sale price) and the fees and closing costs (another 2—5 percent). In this lesson we'll take a look at mortgage loans, closing costs, insurance, and taxes.

Introduce your guest speaker, the real estate agent, who will present Steps 1-4 of this session. A good approach is to do it in a question and answer fashion. For instance, for the Step 1 you could ask the agent: "What are the primary loan sources for first-time buyers?"

STEP 1
Loan Sources for the First-Time Buyer
(10 minutes)

Objective: To introduce students to the various sources for mortgages.

Where you borrow the money for your new home can make a big difference in what it costs to buy a home. The traditional sources are savings and loan (S & L) companies, banks, the government, and private lenders.

When you borrow through a **bank or savings and loan company,** the interest rate is determined by the prevailing interest rate in the economy at that time.

However, there are usually several **government programs** available to aid first-time or low-income home buyers by providing loans at lower interest rates. The most widely known are:
• the Federal Housing Authority (FHA),
• the Veteran's Administration (VA),
• and the Housing and Urban Development (HUD).

Sometimes state or even local governments will allocate funds to aid first-time buyers.

Each of these offer special, lower-interest loans for home buyers. FHA is generally available to most average home buyers. VA is available only to qualifying armed services veterans, and HUD is generally only available in low-income urban areas.

STEP 2
Types of Mortgages (10 minutes)

Objective: To familiarize students with the types of mortgages.

1. **A Few Terms and Definitions**

   Mortgage. This is a type of loan which gives the property to the lender if the borrower is unable to pay off the debt.

   Collateral. The property is the collateral (security or guarantee) for the loan.

   Lien. The contract states that the lender holds a lien (pronounced "lean" and meaning a legal right or bond) on the property.

   Foreclose. The lien holder can foreclose the mortgage (end the contract) and take possession of the property if the buyer cannot make the payments.

2. **Fixed-Rate Mortgages**

   A fixed-rate mortgage is a simple-interest loan using the property as the collateral for the loan. The advantage of a fixed-rate mortgage is that the rates are fixed and cannot be raised. The rates for a fixed rate, thirty-year loan will often be 2—4 percent higher than for an adjustable rate mortgage. As inflation has increased in our economy, fewer home mortgage lenders are willing to lend money for long periods (fifteen to thirty years) at fixed interest rates.

   Their reluctance is understandable if you look at an example. Suppose a lender issued a thirty-year, fixed-rate mortgage at 10 percent, but in five years, because of inflation, the prevailing interest rates went up to 17 percent (as they did in 1981). The lender's earnings are fixed at 10 percent per year for the next twenty-five years. However, payouts (the savings accounts of depositors) are at 17 percent. Fortunately for everyone, interest rates came down. Still, you can see right away that the mortgage lender would have had a real problem if the rates had stayed unusually high.

3. **Adjustable-Rate Mortgages (ARM)**

   To overcome their problem, mortgage lenders have created adjustable-rate mortgages (ARMs). An ARM allows the homeowner's interest rate to be adjusted annually according to a predetermined index (usually the prime lending rate).

   To protect the borrower, most ARMs have a maximum rate of increase each year and a limit on the total maximum rate that can be charged. Usually the limits are a 1 percent increase per year with a maximum rate of 4—6 percent above the initial rate.

Display Visual 8, the "Adjustable Rate Mortgage."

The attractive aspect of ARMs to the borrower is that they are usually given at an initially lower rate than the available fixed-rate mortgages. However, there is no guarantee that they will remain lower—it's somewhat of a gamble.

Anyone considering an ARM would be well advised to budget for increases. A 1 percent increase in a $100,000 mortgage is approximately $63 per month. A 5 percent increase can raise the mortgage payments by over $317 per month!

4. **Fifteen Versus Thirty-year Mortgages**

When purchasing a house, it is often tempting to get the most house for the smallest monthly payment. This usually means spreading the payments out over as long a period as possible—usually over thirty years. Sometimes, this is fine. However, it can be rather shocking to see how much more one must pay in interest by lengthening the mortgage.

Sometimes it is better to accept "less" house, if necessary, so you can get a shorter mortgage.

Have the students turn to Step 2 in their Student Texts to see comparisons between fifteen- and thirty-year mortgages. Point out that a relatively small increase in monthly payments (about 20 percent) cuts the length of payments on a home in half and saves an enormous amount.

Besides the savings of a shorter mortgage, lenders will often offer a fifteen-year, fixed-rate mortgage at 1—1.5 percent below those offered for a thirty-year mortgage. This is because the lender takes less risk of prevailing interest rates rising above a profitable level.

A shorter mortgage would not be advantageous if someone had a thirty-year mortgage at a very low interest rate and could be disciplined enough to invest that $100—$200 per month. But that's a rare arrangement and a difficult discipline.

STEP 3
Closing Costs (5 minutes)

Objective: To enumerate the various closing costs a home buyer should anticipate paying.

Besides needing the money for a down payment on a home, cash is needed to pay the other costs at time of closing. That is why these costs are called "closing costs." They include the following:

1. **Attorney fees.** An attorney should be engaged to represent you at the closing and verify that all documents are correct. Attorney fees normally amount to $150–$250.

2. **Recording costs.** A mortgage note and land deeds must be recorded at the county courthouse where the home is located. The recording fees will normally be $50–100.

3. **Escrow accounts.** Escrow means to place money in the care of a third party for a specific purpose. In a home escrow, the buyer is required to prepay expenses such as insurance and real-estate taxes. Usually at least six month's prepaid taxes and insurance are required to be escrowed at closing. Together these can cost $500–$1,000.

   The seller should also escrow funds for past taxes.

4. **Loan fee points.** "Points," as they are called, are closing costs charged by the lender. A point is 1 percent of the loan amount, and they come in two forms: discount points and loan fee points (or origination fees). Loan fee points are charged by the lender to cover the cost of processing the loan. (A separate loan application fee of $100–$300 may also be charged.)

5. **Discount points.** When loans are offered at relatively low interest rates, the lenders usually charge an up-front fee to get a higher return on your loan. These fees are commonly called "discount points."

   One can easily owe from $2,000–$5,000 at closing beyond the down payment on the home.

STEP 4
Home Insurance (5 minutes)

Objective: To introduce students to the types of insurance the home owner should have.

There are three basic types of insurance that a typical home-owner is faced with selecting: property damage, mortgage insurance, and title insurance.

1. **Property damage insurance.** All mortgage lenders require that you carry insurance to protect the property you have mortgaged. This will pay to repair or replace any physical damage from such things as a fire, flood, earthquake, or storm.

   Additionally, you may elect to cover your furnishings, personal injury, liability, and relocation expenses if your home is damaged.

2. **Mortgage insurance.** This insurance will pay off the remaining mortgage if the insured dies. It is a type of declining life insurance (it declines as the mortgage balance declines).

3. **Title insurance.** When real property (such as a home) is purchased, an attorney hired by the seller does a title search of all the previous owners of the property. This search will show if there are any outstanding claims against it. The attorney then prepares an "abstract," which is a summarized version of all the transactions on the property for as far back as records exist.

STEP 5
Total "Mortgage" Payments (25 minutes)

Objective: To allow the students to calculate what price of a home they could afford and attempt to find examples in their price range.

1. Explain that when estimating the monthly cost of a house, there are at least three things to include.

   P & I (principal and interest). The largest portion of the monthly payment will go to the actual mortgage payment to be applied to the principal (the money borrowed) and interest (the fee for borrowing) of the mortgage. In the early years of a mortgage, the great majority of this money is applied to interest.

   Insurance. Most commonly, the mortgage company will escrow a portion of the monthly payment to cover the annual insurance premiums.

   Property taxes. Similarly, taxes are usually escrowed by the mortgage company and paid annually. Taxes often add $50–$200 per month to the total mortgage payment.

2. Write on the chalkboard these typical monthly costs for a $100,000 mortgage for fifteen years at 10.5 percent interest:

P & I	$1,105
Insurance	50
Taxes	150
TOTAL	$1,305

3. Distribute copies of Form 10, "What Home Can You Buy?" along with copies of the real estate section of a local newspaper. After the students have determined how expensive a home they can afford, have them go through the ads trying to find three options within their price range.

4. Allow time for sharing and discussion as they see what a challenge it is to buy a home. Remind the students that young people today often expect to do in three years what it took their parents fifteen years to do. As a result, many get in trouble by overextending their budget.

This Is Your Life

Applying what they've learned to their present finances. The following appears in the Student Text.

1. Hang in there with recording each expenditure you make under its proper category. Remember to deduct the amount spent from the amount budgeted to give you a running total of what you have left to spend in that category.
2. When or under what conditions do you think young people should begin contributing toward housing if they live in their parents' home?
3. What do your parents think about this?
4. What would be a fair amount in your case?
5. Discover what your costs would be to rent an apartment or house in your community. What are the typical "up-front" charges (i.e., first and last month's rent, security deposit, cleaning fee, etc.)?

FOR ADDITIONAL STUDY

Collect the six months of record keeping done by each student over the past weeks. Make a final check of their calculations to see if they have mastered the process. Schedule a personal meeting with any students who seem to be having problems with any facet of budgeting.

Have the students do the following and then take the quiz (both of which appear in their Student Texts):

Find one person (family) who has purchased a home within the last five years and who is willing to share with you the financial details of their purchase.

What was the purchase price?

What was their down payment?

What were the closing costs apart from the down payment?

What rate of interest do they pay?

How long is their mortgage?

What are the total monthly payments (P & I, insurance, taxes)?

Are there any aspects of the deal they wish they had done differently?

LOOKING FOR WORK

Background:

Managing one's money wisely is the most important element in having All the Money You Need, but it's not the only one. One does need a good job.

Many young people do not know how to go about finding a good job. Some have never had a job. Others who have one came into it without having to search for it. This leaves them handicapped for the future. They may experience long periods of unemployment or under-employment. They may be afraid to try to get a better job. Or they may experience excessive anxiety and depression when they are out of work—a condition that does not leave them in peak condition for finding a new job.

This lesson begins the process of learning how to look for work.

Lesson Aim:
* **To help the students understand the most effective ways to look for work.**

Advance Preparation:

☐ Arrange your classroom so that the students can conveniently divide into pairs for some of the exercises.

☐ If you have not already scheduled a personnel director for next week's lesson and wish to have such a guest speaker, do so now. See the Getting Started section in Lesson 11 for further details on how you should use this resource person.

Getting Started (10 minutes)

Ask those students who have had a regular part-time or full-time job to tell how they found the job. For each new method, write it on the chalkboard:

> Personal referral
> Help wanted ads
> Employment agencies
> Going from business to business
> Noticing a help wanted poster

When you have listed the various approaches, take a poll of how many people have found jobs by each method. (Include yourself in the count.) Although most of these jobs will not be career-level jobs, this exercise will give the students a picture of the variety and value of each job-hunting procedure.

Even if personal referrals don't come out as the most effective method in your informal poll, explain that in a broader cross-section of the working world, personal referrals are often the best method for finding a good job. One can often hear about a position before it is widely advertised. Plus, if the acquaintance is respected, his or her recommendation can be very valuable.

Share the following:

The best budget in the world won't work without the necessary income. However, we have saved the subject of finding a good job until the last. It is seldom the first thing that needs improvement in order to have all the money you need. Wise management of what you have must come first. Too often the average person's first response to money problems is: "If I only had a little more income." As important as a good job is, more income is seldom the biggest problem.

Now that you have learned how to manage what you have, you are ready to talk about looking for work.

STEP 1
Pursuing Help Wanted Ads (5 minutes)

Objective: To help the students thoroughly read help wanted ads.

1. Have the students turn to Step 1 in the Student Text and read through the sample help wanted ads. You can have the students take turns reading the ads aloud or have them read them silently.

2. Explain that it is important to read want ads thoroughly and reply exactly as the ad says. An employer often gets his or her initial impression by the way an applicant answers the ad. A person who can't follow the directions given in the ad probably won't follow directions on the job.

3. After the ads have been read, ask the following questions:
   1. Which job or jobs would be suitable for a full-time student? (Ads number 2, 4, 5, 8, 10, and 11.)
   2. Why would ad number 9 not be suitable for a student? (The age requirement for a taxi license is usually twenty-one or older.)
   3. What do you think "commission only" in ad number 6 means? (The employee earns no salary, only a percentage of each sale. No sales, no income.)

STEP 2
Using Employment Agencies (5 minutes)

Objective: To help the students consider some of the pros and cons of employment agencies.

1. Explain the following:
   Sometimes jobs offered in the want ads are placed by an employment agency. Private employment agencies work in two ways. When they list a position and say, "Fee paid,"

this means that the employer will pay all the associated fees.

However, if "fee paid" is not mentioned in the want ad, it is likely that the applicant will have to pay the agency for finding him or her a job. This fee usually is a certain percentage of the employee's first month's pay. The fee varies from agency to agency.

Sometimes when you can't find employment on your own, an agency is the best way to seek help. However, you need to be sure you have exhausted all your own resources before paying an agency to find you a job.

2. Ask the following questions:
   1. Which job in the previous ads would be through an agency? (Ad number 8.)
   2. Who would most likely pay the expenses of the agency? (Probably the applicant.)
   3. When is it best to use an agency? (When you have exhausted your resources.)
      Why? (Because they charge a fee.)
3. Point out that state employment agencies don't charge fees.

STEP 3
Developing Your Confidence (20 minutes)

Objective: To guide the students in developing their job skills profile.

1. Divide the students into pairs. Each partner should interview the other person for five minutes, using the questions on Step 3 of the Student Text to develop a marketable skills profile of the other person. They should take notes on one another and deliver the "profile" to their partner when the time is up. Call "time" after the first five minutes and after the second five-minute segment.
2. Then have each class member write an ad for a service he or she could offer. It should be done in the style of the ads in the Student Text and based on the skills profile taken by their partner. Allow about five minutes to write the ads.
3. Reconvene the class and have several students share their ads.

STEP 4
Answering an Ad (20 minutes)

Objective: To allow the students to practice presenting themselves well in making a phone inquiry to set up a job interview.

FOR ADDITIONAL STUDY

Have the students take the quiz in the Student book.

1. Draw the students' attention to the tips in their books for answering ads by phone and mail.

2. Divide the class into pairs again to simulate a telephone conversation. One partner takes the part of the employer and the other is the prospective employee.

   Each student should choose one of the ads from Step 1 in the Student Text as the job that he or she is applying for. The "employer" should take notes on every aspect of the job seeker's presentation: alertness, politeness, suitability of skills for the job, etc.

3. After a five-minute conversation, call "time" and have each "employer" say whether he or she would be interested in setting up a personal interview with the "applicant." Instruct the employer to suggest any improvements which could enhance the applicant's contact.

4. Have the partners exchange roles and repeat the exercise.

This Is Your Life

Applying what they've learned to their present finances. The following appears in the Student Text.

1. Based on two to three months of keeping track of your income and expenses, do you need to:
   - get a job?
   - work more hours in your present job?
   - change jobs?
   - Why or why not?

2. If you feel you need a new job, decide the following:
   a. What kind of job you want.
   b. How to locate such a job.
   c. How much per hour you need to make.
   d. How many hours you can work per week.

WRITING A SHARP RESUMÉ

Background:

The resumé is often the first impression an employer has of an applicant. So, a well-planned and well-written resumé can be the tool which leads to an interview and then a job. Young people who cannot represent themselves and their skills effectively in a one- or two-page resumé will not get further consideration for many positions.

This lesson will provide the elements of writing a good resumé.

Lesson Aim:
- **To guide students in writing a good resumé.**

Advance Preparation

☐ Check that the personnel director you invited will be coming for this lesson as your guest speaker. Confirm time and directions, etc. Discuss with the speaker how you would like him or her to contribute.

☐ Prepare an overhead transparency of Visual 9, "The Resumé Format."

☐ Have available for each student a copy of Form 11, "Creating Your Resumé."

Getting Started (20 minutes)

Introduce the guest speaker, who will then lead a discussion about the kinds of things a personnel director looks for when seeking a new employee. This presentation can cover information from the previous lesson, this one, and the next lesson. To help move the discussion along you might ask the following questions:

- How do you find most of the employees your company hires?
- Is there any difference in the way you recruit entry-level workers?
- What is the first way you eliminate unsuitable applicants (the way they respond on the phone, the way they appear when you first meet them, their past experience, etc.)?
- How often do you check applicants' references, and how important are references?
- What do you look for in an applicant's resumé? What kinds of resumés turn you off?
- What are the most important elements in an interview with a prospective employee?
- What kind of follow-up is appropriate for a potential employee?
- What are the most critical things for a new employee to do to keep his or her new job?

Allow time for the students to ask questions before thanking the guest speaker for his or her time and moving on with the lesson.

STEP 1
Rules for Preparing Your Resumé (10 minutes)

Objective: To identify some guidelines for preparing a good resumé.

1. Explain the purpose of the resumé:

   The traditional and best way for a job applicant to communicate his or her background, abilities, and experience to a potential employer is through the "resumé," a written summary of the work-related assets he or she can bring to a job. A good resumé is usually one page in length (never more than two pages). It should outline one's education, experience, interests, skills, and sometimes the applicant's job objectives.

   The resumé is often the first tool employers use to screen unwanted applicants (similar to a phone call). So a well-planned and well-written resumé can be what gets one an interview and ultimately a job.

2. Share the following guidelines for a good resumé:

   1) **Your resumé should be brief.** Most people don't read them word for word, anyway. Think of it as a brief advertisement for you.

   2) **Your resumé should be easy to read.** When typing your resumé, use columns, margins, capital letters and other devices to make your resumé attractive. Just don't try to be cute.

   3) **Job objectives are optional** for the first-time job seeker.

   4) **List courses you have taken** which contribute to your qualifications for the job. Also, mention an area of emphasis if it contributes to your qualification. Keep this listing brief.

   5) **Condense your listing of past jobs** as briefly as possible.

   6) **Emphasize the skills you have developed.**

   7) **Be ready to supply references** who can speak well of your working abilities and personal characteristics.

STEP 2
The Resume Format (10 minutes)

Objective: To help students examine the format in which the resumé information should be arranged.

1. Display with the overhead projector Visual 9, "The Resumé Format," and go over the sections with the students. The Student book has an expanded explanation of each component.
2. Share the following information:

   What Not to Include in a Resume:
   1) The salary you desire. This should be discussed in an interview.
   2) Your age, your marital status, and children.
   3) Any handicaps you may have. If you are seeking a position which you honestly believe you can handle despite a handicap, you need not mention a handicap.

   Specifics of the Format
   1) Type the resumé, and make it free of spelling or grammatical errors.
   2) Leave space between sections of the resumé— especially areas you want to stand out. Remember, your resumé advertises you.
   3) Try to limit the resumé to one page or two at the most.
   4) Having your resumé professionally printed is desirable, especially when you are applying for a full-time position. Never send a carbon or a poor quality photocopy.

STEP 3
Designing Your Resume (15 minutes)

Objective: To guide the students in collecting the basic elements they would need in preparing an effective resumé.

Distribute copies of Form 11, "Creating Your Resumé," to the students and have them fill out the form. The Student Text shows a sample resumé. If you intend to assign the For Additional Study section at the end of the lesson, this page will be the basis for writing a resumé.

STEP 4
Writing a Cover Letter (5 minutes)

Objective: To inform the students of the purpose and proper design of a good cover letter.

FOR ADDITIONAL STUDY

Have the students do the following (which appears in their Student Texts):

1. From your information sheet on Form 11, "Creating Your Resumé," type up a resumé in the best form you can.
2. Write a cover letter to an imaginary company to go with your resumé.
3. Have two people who are good writers read your resumé and cover letter, suggesting how to condense and clarify what you have said. Don't include any unnecessary words or phrases.

1. Teach the following:

    A cover letter should be placed on top of your resumé to communicate more personally with the potential employer and make sure you are considered for the specific job which you want.

    An employer may be considering applicants for more than one job. For the most part, resumés look alike. Because of this, applicants sometimes are not given careful consideration, especially when several are under consideration. Sometimes the cover letter is the element that catches his or her eye.

    Your cover letter should draw attention to your resumé. It should be done in a businesslike form as described in the last lesson. It should be brief, and yet explain who you are and why you want to be considered for the job. It should not exceed one short page.

2. Refer the students to the Student Text for a sample cover letter.

This Is Your Life

Applying what they've learned to their present finances. The following appears in the Student Text.

1. Continue with recording your actual expenses in your appropriate budget category.
2. If you are seriously looking for a (new) job, send copies of the resumé you prepared for this lesson to actual companies/ places of business where you would like to apply. Try to discover the name of the personnel manager in charge of hiring, and address your cover letter to him or her.

THE WINNING JOB INTERVIEW

Background:

Stage fright doesn't strike only when one is standing before a crowd. One of its most costly attacks can come in the job interview when the applicant sits across the desk from a potential employer.

The intensity and devastation of these fears can be alleviated by three things:

(1) knowing what to expect in the job interview,

(2) being prepared to respond properly, and

(3) practice.

Advance Preparation:

☐ Arrange your classroom so that the students can conveniently divide into pairs for Step 2.

Getting Started (5 minutes)

Share the following:

The job interview is the final and most important step involved in being hired for a job. If your application has been reviewed, your resumé and contents of your cover letter read, and you are asked to come in for an interview, then you are a serious candidate for the job. However, remember that usually several others are also trying for the same position.

Merely because you are selected for a job interview does not guarantee you a job. Sometimes the interview will convince both you and the employer that this is not the job for you.

If you do not get the first job you apply for, don't become discouraged. You can learn from each experience, even the negative ones. It is not unusual for a company to interview twenty people for a single job. Even though you may feel the job is perfect for you, the interviewer may not, or he or she may fail to recognize your abilities.

Remember that though a good initial impression doesn't automatically guarantee you the job, a bad initial impression will practically guarantee that you will not get the job.

The interview may be the potential employer's first look at you. Everything about you is important during this time. You need to be concerned about your personal physical appearance, but even more, your attitude will announce whether you can work willingly under this employer's leadership. Remember why you are at the interview: to demonstrate that you can do a specific job for the employer.

Lesson Aim:
- **To help the students consider elements of effective job interviews.**
- **To allow students to practice being interviewed for a job.**

STEP 1
So, You've Got the Interview (5 minutes)

Objective: To prepare students for a successful interview.

As you share the following suggestions for preparing for an interview, write the main points on the chalkboard. Ask the students for their suggestions about each point. You can add whatever points the students don't mention.

1. **Be prepared.** You need to be able to answer all questions about yourself, your background, and even your family life. Be specific and brief when answering questions. Don't, under any circumstances, exaggerate about your background. Have an extra copy of your resumé with you, should it have been misplaced.

2. **Do some homework.** If it is possible, learn a little about the company before your interview. What is the business? How is this business transacted? Be prepared by learning as much about the potential employer as possible. This will show your interest in the company's well-being.

3. **Watch your appearance.** Good grooming is a must. Most employers are impressed with a conservative and clean-cut look. Don't dress too casually or try to be "sexy." Forget blue jeans, fad shirts, and heavy makeup. Dark colors are the most conservative, and greens, browns, and rust colors are good for women. Shine your shoes and spit out the gum. If you aren't familiar with proper dress for a particular job you are going after, seek out help in this area before going to the interview.

4. **Be on time.** Never keep an interviewer waiting for you. If there is any possibility of a transportation delay (traffic jam, late bus, etc.), leave early enough to compensate. If you get to your destination fifteen to thirty minutes early, that's much better than arriving breathlessly at the last moment or being late. You can wait in your car or walk around the block during the extra time and get to the company's door about ten minutes ahead of time.

STEP 2
During the Interview (30 minutes)

Objective: To help students practice a simulated interview.

1. As you share the following suggestions for making a good first impression in an interview, write the main points on the

chalkboard. Ask students to tell why they think each point is important.

1) **Relax.** Wait for the interviewer to tell you where to sit. Look at the interviewer and make eye contact when he or she is talking and you are answering. The first few minutes of an interview should be spent in getting acquainted.

2) **Listen.** Be careful to listen to the name of the one interviewing you, if you don't know it beforehand. The sweetest sound to anyone's ear is the sound of his or her own name. Listen precisely to questions or comments made by the interviewer. Don't add small talk or chitchat. Don't tell funny jokes.

3) **Think** before you speak, and then answer all questions honestly and completely. Avoid cryptic yes-and-no answers to questions that can be answered more fully.

4) **Let the interviewer introduce salary.** Don't try to discuss money until the interviewer brings it up. The interviewer knows that it's important to you and will discuss it with you if you are being seriously considered. (The only time you should bring it up is if you are offered the job without money being mentioned. Obviously, you shouldn't say yes until there is a clear commitment on your wages.)

5) **Watch what you say and do.** Don't use slang or make uncomplimentary comments about former employers or co-workers. Any old resentments you express will cause the interviewer to suspect that you will develop the same attitudes toward him or her. Don't shake hands unless the interviewer prompts it. Don't accept an interviewer's offer of refreshments unless he or she takes refreshments, too, and urges your participation. Don't collapse into the chair or put your feet on any furniture. Don't comb your hair, file your nails, etc., during an interview.

6) **Ask questions.** If you have questions, ask them. Don't walk away from an interview and "wish" you had asked.

7) **Be gracious as you leave.** Many potential jobs are lost as the interviewee walks out the door. This can easily happen if you let down your guard or don't display good manners during the last minutes of an interview. Sometimes this is the result of becoming too comfortable or familiar. Also, if you are not offered the job on the spot, it is tempting to become disappointed. Make sure you do not express a sour or flippant attitude that will turn off an employer. Keep your attitude positive; remain polite and expectant. Don't beg, plead, or cry to get the job.

2. Divide the students into pairs and have them role-play an interview for a "job of their choice." They should name any job they want and believe they are currently qualified to fill. One partner should play the employer and the other the job applicant.

3. After five minutes, call "time." Allow a few minutes for the "employer" to say whether he or she would have hired the applicant and why or why not.

4. Then have the partners change roles and repeat the process. This interview should be more "professional" than the phone dialogs in Lesson 11.

   If you assigned the For Additional Study from the previous lesson, then the students should use the resumés they created. If they did not create resumés, then they should use their filled out copies of Form 11, "Creating Your Resumé," which contains the primary information.

STEP 3
The Follow-Up (5 minutes)

Objective: To outline the appropriate way to follow up a job interview.

1. Reconvene the class, and point out that a job offer will seldom be made during an interview.

   Usually several people are being interviewed, and the employer wants to select the best person for the job. Therefore, one cannot expect a direct answer to whether or not one has gotten the job at the interview. Usually the answer will come through a phone call or letter within one to two weeks after the interview. If the applicant hasn't heard by that time (or the time designated by the interviewer), it is appropriate to call and check on the process.

2. Suggest that sending a thank-you note to the interviewer is gracious.

   A note is unlikely to appear too anxious if it expresses thanks for the time and consideration given. It will make a good impression, and it will keep the applicant on the mind of the potential employer.

3. Remind the students that once they get a job, how well they do is dependent on additional skills.

   Job success skills include timeliness, self-discipline, courteousness, training, etc. Encourage them to remember that what they do on the job and how they do it will speak more clearly than anything they have said about themselves in their applications, resumés, or interviews.

STEP 4
Wrap Up (15 minutes)

Objective: To conclude the course with a time of review and evaluation.

1. Have the students turn to Step 4 in their Student Text and take the review quiz printed there.
2. When they finish, go over the answers in class, or if it is important to grade the quiz, collect each student's workbook.
3. Congratulate the students and thank them for participating in the course with you. Invite comments about what has impressed them most about managing money.

This Is Your Life

Applying what they've learned to their present finances. The following appears in the Student Text

Evaluate the records you have kept of your actual income and expenses for the past three months.

1. What changes have projecting a budget and keeping records of actual expenses made on your spending patterns, if any?
2. What changes would you like to make?
3. What needs to happen to make those changes possible?

FOR ADDITIONAL STUDY

Assign your students to role play a job interview (following the instructions in the Student Text).

GIVING TO GOD

Background:

Giving primarily benefits the giver. Giving reminds us of our relationship to God, with Him as our Lord and Master and us as His servants and stewards.

Confusion on this perspective has far broader implications than making it hard for the local church to operate financially. Faithfulness in such a small thing as money is a prerequisite to being entrusted with the riches and responsibilities of God's Kingdom.

It is important for young people to learn the broad variety of ways they can give to the Lord. Even those who are convinced of giving a tithe to the church may not realize that they have other God-ordained responsibilities. Also, they may not understand that the Bible speaks of multiple levels of giving which go beyond the strict tithe.

A failure to comprehend these truths could leave people in the position of the Pharisees. Jesus condemned them because they technically tithed but neglected the attitude and actions of mercy and justice.

Lesson Aim:
- **To help the students understand why God wants us to give and how our giving can be "giving to God."**

Advance Preparation:

☐ Have your students bring Bibles for this lesson, or provide Bibles for the class.

☐ Arrange the classroom so that during Step 4 the students can write privately without worrying about someone seeing their responses.

Getting Started (5 minutes)

Begin the class by explaining that this lesson is about giving, the first category on Form 1, the "Monthly Income and Expenses." Ask, "Why do you think most Christians give a portion of their money away?" Write their answers on the chalkboard without evaluating them.

Tell the students that one goal of this lesson is to discover the biblical answers to why Christians should give a portion of their money.

As the lesson proceeds, put a check by each of the reasons for giving as you or the students emphasize them during the lesson.

STEP 1
Why Should the Christian Give? (15 minutes)

Objective: To help students recognize that giving reminds us that God is the true owner of everything, and we are His stewards.

1. Ask two volunteers to look up and read aloud 1 Corinthians 6:19, 20, and Romans 12:1. Then ask, "What do these verses tell us about being our own masters?" (We belong to God.)

2. Next ask volunteers to read Psalm 50:10-12 and 1 Chronicles 29:14-16. Explain that this last passage is part of a prayer by King David after the people of Israel contributed large offerings to build the Temple. Then ask the class to answer the following questions:
   • Who is the true owner of everything? (God.)
   • What is our basic relationship to all material things? (Temporary residents, wanderers or "tenants," as the NASB says in 1 Chronicles 29:15.)
   • Does God need our money? (No.)

3. Point out that these passages show that all we are and all we have belongs to God. He has allowed us to be the stewards or managers over our lives and possessions.

4. Ask, "Why do you think God has entrusted us with the management of our lives and the things He has put into our hands?"

5. Summarize the Parable of the Talents (Matt. 25:14-30). Have a student read Matthew 25:21. Then ask, "Why do you think God does not do everything Himself?" or "Why did He not make robots that unthinkingly do His bidding?" (God wants us to mature and grow in our ability to be servants and co-workers in His Kingdom. Therefore He gives us responsibility.)

6. Present the following points:
   1) A faithful steward or manager never forgets who the true owner is. Still, we easily forget that all we are and have belongs to God.
   2) Giving to God a portion of what we have is the method God has set up to remind us that we are not self-made creatures and that all we have has actually been given to us.
   3) When we try to keep everything for ourselves, we reveal a serious problem in our perspective on life. We are looking at ourselves as owners, not managers.
   4) When we look at money and possessions as ours, we inevitably look at every other aspect of our life the same way. We see ourselves as being in charge. We begin to think of God as our servant, there to help us when we call upon Him. Rather, we should see ourselves as God's servants, ready always to do His will. That is what it means to call Him "Lord." Lord means ruler, owner, sovereign, king.
   5) Giving to God is so important because it reminds us who He is and who we are. Giving also shows what our relation-

ship should be to the things He has allowed us to manage in His name.

STEP 2
How Do We Give to God? (15 minutes)

Objective: To help the students identify several ways in which they can "give to God" by meeting the needs of others.

1. Ask, "If God owns everything and therefore doesn't personally need anything, how can we give anything of significance to Him?" (The answer can be found in the way God has set up the world. While it is possible for God to shower manna from heaven to feed the hungry, that is not His usual method of meeting people's needs. Usually, when someone is hungry and unable to provide for himself or herself, God touches the heart of another person to share.)

2. Have the students look up the following scriptures and match them with the ways that we can give to God by meeting others' needs. These scriptures and a scrambled list of ways of giving are in their books:

   1. Malachi 3:10a   (Funding church programs.)
   2. 1 Timothy 5:17,18   (Support for ministers.)
   3. 2 Corinthians 8:13-15   (Sharing with Christians.)
   4. 1 Timothy 5:8   (Helping needy relatives.)
   5. Matthew 25:37-40   (Giving to the poor.)
   6. Luke 10:1-7   (Supporting missionaries.)

3. Conclude this matching activity by reminding students of Jesus' words in Matthew 25:40: ". . . whatever you did . . . , you did for Me." So, giving as God wants us to give is counted as giving to Him.

STEP 3
Four Levels of Giving (20 minutes)

Objective: To introduce the students to four levels of giving and show how God will care for them as they practice all four.

1. Divide the class into four sections. Assign the students in each section one of the four levels of giving described in the Student Text. Instruct them to read their assigned section and be ready to explain to the class what the level of giving involves.

2. After three or four minutes, call on volunteers who read about the tithe, asking them to describe that giving level. The Student Text provides the following information:

A. **Giving the Tithe.** The word "tithe" literally means a tenth. It is the least amount God ever asked His people to give.

The first time we see any mention of a tithe in the Bible is in Genesis 14:20. Abraham was returning from a great battle when he was met by Melchizedek. Many Bible scholars believe that Melchizedek was actually Jesus Christ, Himself. Abraham certainly recognized that Melchizedek represented the most high God. Thus, Abraham gave to him a tithe, or tenth.

Why would Abraham, with all his warriors by his side, give away a tenth of all that he had to a priest? In doing so, Abraham acknowledged God's ownership of all that he had. That was the purpose of the tithe, and it remains the same today.

1) Have a student read aloud Malachi 3:10.
2) Ask, "What instructions and what promise does God give in this verse?" (God instructs us to give the tithe, and He promises to bless those who tithe freely.)
3) Instruct everyone to find Malachi 3:6-12 and discover why God gave the people this reminder. Ask these questions:

   • What was happening in their lives?
   • What does the passage say would be the consequences of giving the whole tithe?
   • What would logically be the consequences of not doing so?

4) Call on volunteers who read about obedient giving to describe what they found about that level of giving. The Student Text says:

B. **Giving out of Obedience.** In Matthew 23:23, Jesus scolded the Pharisees. Even though they carefully tithed such minor things as the herbs from their garden, they "neglected the more important matters of the law—justice and mercy and faithfulness." While He affirmed their tithing, He said that the Law called them to go further.

In verse 25, He said that they were "full of greed and self-indulgence." Obedience to God calls for something more than legalistic observance of tithing, because it is possible to technically tithe to God and be cruel to people in need.

1) Point out that Jesus clearly explained what God expects in the way of true justice and mercy. Have a student read Matthew 25:34-36, then ask:

   • "According to this passage, How had this giving to

Jesus been accomplished?" (His true followers gave to those in need.)
- "What would be an obedient response when you encounter someone in need?"
- "What does this say to you about the kinds of giving you should be doing?"

2) Call on those who read about giving from abundance. Ask them to describe that level of giving. The Student Text says:

C. Giving Out of Our Abundance. Sometimes we may be saving for a legitimate future need such as education, retirement, a home, etc.. But along the way we encounter someone or some worthy project where the need is greater. At that point, if we choose to give out of our savings, we are giving out of our abundance. This is usually very difficult because it means giving up something we truly desire.

1) Have a student read Luke 12:15-21. Ask these questions:
- What is this story teaching about saving for the future?
- Why are riches so dangerous?

2) Call on those who read about sacrificial giving. Ask them to describe what they learned. The Student Text says:

D. Sacrificial Giving. Sacrificial giving means giving up a "need" to help someone who may have even greater needs. John the Baptist described this attitude in Luke 3:11: "The man with two tunics should share with him who has none, and the one who has food should do the same."

1) Have a student read Luke 21:1-4.

2) Ask, "If you give up a need, won't you end up suffering want?" (That's a good question, and Jesus answered it directly. He said in Matthew 6:33, "But seek first his kingdom and his righteousness; and all these things will be given to you as well." The "things" Jesus mentioned were the basics of life—the food and shelter and clothing that we all need.)

3) Ask, "Does this mean that Christians will never be poor?" Be prepared to respond to student comments:

Some of us will be poor. However, there's a difference between being poor and suffering want. One can be technically poor and have all the money needed. God stations His people as witnesses in every level of life—from poor to rich. One of our missions in life is to show that God's grace is sufficient no matter what our experience—even when it's hard. As Paul said, "But he said to me, 'My grace is sufficient for you, for my power is made perfect in weakness.' Therefore I will boast all the more gladly about my weaknesses, so that Christ's power may rest on me" (2 Corinthians 12:9).

4) Ask, "Can we be lazy, therefore, and expect God to feed us?" (Paul set down the rule in 2 Thessalonians 3:10: "If a man will not work, he shall not eat." Laziness is not consistent with righteousness.)

5) Conclude this study by emphasizing God's promise to care for the righteous, to meet our basic needs.

King David said, "I was young, and now I am old, yet I have never seen the righteous forsaken or their children begging bread" (Psalm 37:25). Similarly, Solomon declared, "The Lord does not let the righteous go hungry" (Proverbs 10:3).

6) Call attention to the paragraphs in the Student Text about times of disaster, famine and war, in which *everyone* suffers.

Christians are not exempt from the consequences of living in a world marred by sin. Repeatedly in Scripture we read of God's people enduring great hardships along with everyone else. We even read of suffering which came specifically because they were obeying God: "I have labored and toiled and have often gone without sleep; I have known hunger and thirst and have often gone without food; I have been cold and naked" (2 Corinthians 11:27).

Paul assured us that no hardship will ever take us out of God's loving presence: "Who shall separate us from the love of Christ? Shall trouble or hardship or persecution or famine or nakedness or danger or sword?... No, in all things we are more than conquerors through him who loved us" (Romans 8:35-37).

STEP 4
Making a Commitment (5 minutes)

Objective: To encourage the students declare their surrender to the Lord and commit themselves to a regular pattern of giving.

Have the students work privately to complete Step 4 in their Student Texts.

This Is Your Life

Applying what they've learned to their present finances. The following appears in the Student Text.

1. While it's a drag remembering to write down what you spend, it's a crucial step in learning to manage your money now.

2. In this lesson you considered making a commitment to set aside a percentage of your money each month for God's work. If so, will you need to adjust the percentages or amounts you've allotted to other categories? Remember, all categories must add up to 100 percent of your NSI.

FOR ADDITIONAL STUDY

Have the students do the following (which appears in their Student Texts):

1. Onto the end of your last month's budget records, incorporate the following variations:
   a. Your washing machine broke down—beyond repair. You must purchase a new one at a budget-busting $400.
   b. If you have been practicing charitable giving, you have just received a tax refund because of overpayment of your income taxes. (Be sure to use a "bank deposit" for recording your tax refund into your records.) The government allows you to deduct authorized charitable giving from your gross income before calculating your net taxable income. Figure out what your refund is this way:
      1. Multiply your monthly charitable giving by twelve.
      2. Subtract this amount from your gross annual income.
      3. Multiply Line 2 by your tax percentage rate. (See Appendix A.)
      4. Multiply your old monthly tax by twelve (See Form 1.)
      5. Subtract Line 3 from Line 4. This is the amount of your refund.

Note: In real life it is not this simple nor would you receive this much of a refund. The reason is that your Social Security contribution is figured before deductions, while only your other taxes can benefit from allowable deductions in calculating your net taxable income.)

2. Have students review this session by taking the quiz in the "For Additional Study" section of their books.

Monthly Income and Expenses

Job Name _____ # _____

Annual Income _____

Monthly Income _____

LESS

1. **Charitable Contributions** _____
2. **Tax** _____

NET SPENDABLE INCOME _____

3. **Housing #_____ (30%)** _____
   Mortgage (rent) _____
   Insurance _____
   Taxes _____
   Electricity _____
   Gas _____
   Water _____
   Sanitation _____
   Telephone _____
   Maintenance _____
   Other _____

4. **Food (17%)** _____

5. **Auto(s) # _____ (15%)** _____
   Payments _____
   Gas & Oil _____
   Insurance _____
   License _____
   Taxes _____
   Maint./Repair/
     Replacement _____

6. **Insurance (5%)** _____
   Life# ____ _____
   Medical# ____ _____

   Other# ____ _____

7. **Debts (5%)** _____
   Credit Cards _____
   Loans & Notes _____
   Other _____

8. **Enter. & Recreation (7%)** _____
   Eating Out _____
   Trips _____
   Babysitters _____
   Activities# ____ _____
   Vacation# ____ _____

   Other _____

9. **Clothing #_____ (5%)** _____

10. **Savings (5%)** _____

11. **Medical Expenses (5%)** _____
    Doctor _____
    Dental _____
    Drugs _____
    Other _____

12. **Miscellaneous (6%)** _____
    Toiletry, cosmetics _____
    Beauty, barber _____
    Laundry, cleaning _____
    Allowances,
      lunches _____
    Subscriptions _____
    Gifts
      (incl. Christmas) _____
    Special Education _____
    Cash _____
    Other _____

TOTAL EXPENSES _____

Net Spendable Income _____

Difference _____

Division of Pay

PER YEAR $ _____   DIVISION OF PAY
PER MONTH $ _____   PER PAY PERIOD $ _____

MONTHLY PAYMENT CATEGORY	$_____ 1st PAY PERIOD	$_____ 2nd PAY PERIOD
1. Charitable Contributions		
2. Taxes		
NET SPENDABLE INCOME (PER MONTH)	$_____	$_____
3. Housing		
4. Food		
5. Automobile(s)		
6. Insurance		
7. Debts		
8. Enter. & Recreation		
9. Clothing		
10. Savings		
11. Medical		
12. Miscellaneous		
TOTALS (Items 3 through 12)	$_____	$_____

Individual Account Sheets

ACCOUNT NAME	MONTHLY ALLOCATION	1st PAY PERIOD	2nd PAY PERIOD

DATE	TRANSACTION	DEPOSIT	W/DRAW	BALANCE

Bank Deposits

BANK DEPOSIT

MONTH: _____ 1st: _____ 2nd: _____

Deposit: _____

Category: 1. $_____
    2. $_____
    3. $_____
    4. $_____
    5. $_____
    6. $_____
    7. $_____
    8. $_____
    9. $_____
   10. $_____
   11. $_____
   12. $_____

       Total: _____

BANK DEPOSIT

MONTH: _____ 1st: _____ 2nd: _____

Deposit: _____

Category: 1. $_____
    2. $_____
    3. $_____
    4. $_____
    5. $_____
    6. $_____
    7. $_____
    8. $_____
    9. $_____
   10. $_____
   11. $_____
   12. $_____

       Total: _____

BANK DEPOSIT

MONTH: _____ 1st: _____ 2nd: _____

Deposit: _____

Category: 1. $_____
    2. $_____
    3. $_____
    4. $_____
    5. $_____
    6. $_____
    7. $_____
    8. $_____
    9. $_____
   10. $_____
   11. $_____
   12. $_____

       Total: _____

BANK DEPOSIT

MONTH: _____ 1st: _____ 2nd: _____

Deposit: _____

Category: 1. $_____
    2. $_____
    3. $_____
    4. $_____
    5. $_____
    6. $_____
    7. $_____
    8. $_____
    9. $_____
   10. $_____
   11. $_____
   12. $_____

       Total: _____

Blank Checks

CATEGORY # _____   CHECK # _____

_____ 19_____

PAY TO THE
ORDER OF _____ $ _____

_____ DOLLARS

BANK OF _____

_____

CATEGORY # _____   CHECK # _____

_____ 19_____

PAY TO THE
ORDER OF _____ $ _____

_____ DOLLARS

BANK OF _____

_____

CATEGORY # _____   CHECK # _____

_____ 19_____

PAY TO THE
ORDER OF _____ $ _____

_____ DOLLARS

BANK OF _____

_____

Checking Account Reconciliation

Month: _____

A. Add up all your deposits (from your deposit slips, not your ledger). . . . _____

B. Add up all the checks you have written. (Use your actual checks, not your ledger). . . . . _____

C. Subtract B from A. . . . . _____

D. Multiply the number of checks you have written by ten cents. . . . . _____

E. Subtract D from C to find your *Bank Balance*. _____

Checking Account Reconciliation

Month: _____

A. Add up all your deposits (from your deposit slips, not your ledger). . . . _____

B. Add up all the checks you have written. (Use your actual checks, not your ledger). . . . . _____

C. Subtract B from A. . . . . _____

D. Multiply the number of checks you have written by ten cents. . . . . _____

E. Subtract D from C to find your *Bank Balance*. _____

Loan Applications

1. PURPOSE: _____
_____

   Month: _____   Amount: _____   Payment: _____
_____
_____
_____
   Approval: _____   _____
_____

2. PURPOSE: _____
_____

   Month: _____   Amount: _____   Payment: _____
_____
_____
_____
   Approval: _____   _____
_____

3. PURPOSE: _____
_____

   Month: _____   Amount: _____   Payment: _____
_____
_____
_____
   Approval: _____   _____
_____

4. PURPOSE: _____
_____

   Month: _____   Amount: _____   Payment: _____
_____
_____
_____
   Approval: _____   _____

Insurance Needs Worksheet

PRESENT INCOME PER YEAR

_____
Line 1

INCOME AVAILABLE

Social Security _____

Investments _____

_____ Total = _____
Line 2

ADDITIONAL INCOME REQUIRED TO SUPPORT FAMILY

(Line 1 - Line 2) = _____
Line 3

INSURANCE REQUIRED TO PROVIDE THE NEEDED INCOME

(Line 3 x 10) = _____
Line 4

LUMP SUM REQUIREMENTS (OPTIONAL)

Debt Payments _____

Funeral Costs _____

Education Costs _____

_____ _____

_____ _____

Total = _____
Line 5

TOTAL FUNDS REQUIRED

(Line 4 + 5) _____
Line 6

TOTAL INSURANCE NEEDED

(Line 6) = _____

Car Selection Worksheet

1. What type of car do you need (two-door, four-door, truck, etc.)? _____
   _____

2. Establish your maximum price range based on your budget by doing the following:

   A. Set the trade-in value of your "present" car at 50 percent of the cash you were allotted for a car at the beginning of the course. (Sorry, that's just the nature of depreciation.) _____

   B. How much can you afford in monthly payments according to "Payments" on Form 1, "Monthly Income and Expenses," under Category 5? _____

   C. Divide line B by $3.50, then multiply this amount by $100. (Payments at 15 percent over three years are approximately $3.50 per $100.) _____

   D. Add line A and line C to determine your maximum price range.

   _____

3. What equipment do you need (air conditioning, automatic, power steering, etc.)?
   _____

4. Using the automotive ads (by dealers) and the classified ads (from private individuals) in the available newspapers, find three cars in your price range that would fill your needs. Where mileage is not given, estimate 12,000 per year unless the ad says "low mileage", then estimate 10,000. (The "rating" is determined in the next step.)

Type	Year	Mileage	Price	Rating

5. Look up those three cars by make and model in a consumer products rating service such as *Consumer Reports* magazine's "Annual Auto Issue" or their "Buying Guide." Rate the cars by placing a "1" by the best, a "2" by the next best, and a "3" by the poorest value.

6. What is *your* first choice? _____

7. If you chose something other than the "first" rated car, explain why. (For instance: price, age, mileage, or personal preference.) _____
   _____

What Home Can You Buy?

The monthly payments on a 10.5 percent, thirty-year mortgage average $9.15 per $1,000 of borrowed money. To find a home you can buy, work through the following steps.

1. List your NSI from Form 1, your "Monthly Income and Expenses." _____

2. Calculate 30 percent of this amount to determine how much you can spend on housing. (.30 x your NSI.) _____

3. Of course, not all of that money can be used for mortgage payments. Utilities, insurance, and taxes must come out of it, too. Assume 60 percent of your housing allotment can go for the mortgage. (.60 x Line 2) _____

4. To calculate how much you can borrow for this monthly payment (assuming a 10.5 percent mortgage over thirty years), divide Line 3 by $9.15 and then multiply that amount by 1,000. This is the size of a mortgage that you can afford. _____

5. Add to Line 4 the cash you saved for a home. It was given in Lesson 1 with your job description. _____

6. Subtract $3,000 from Line 5 as an estimated amount for closing costs. This is the price of a home you can afford. _____

7. Look in the real estate section of a local newspaper and see if you can find three homes or condominiums for this amount. List their price and a brief description below.

_____

_____

_____

Creating Your Resumé

Fill in the information below.

NAME: _____

Address: _____

City/State/Zip: _____

Phone: _____

EDUCATION: _____

_____

_____

_____

_____

_____

_____

_____

EXPERIENCE: _____

_____

_____

_____

_____

_____

_____

_____

_____

_____

_____

_____

**ACTIVITIES/
INTERESTS:** _____

_____

_____

_____

_____

_____

_____

REFERENCES: _____

_____

_____

JOB ASSIGNMENTS

— — — — — — — — — — — CUT APART — — — — — — — — — — —

1. ATTORNEY
Salary: $32,000
Tax Rate: 30% ($800 per month)

Twice-monthly paychecks (taxes withheld): $933.33 each

Cash down payments available:
  House = $15,000; Auto = $8,000

— — — — — — — — — — — CUT APART — — — — — — — — — — —

2. DENTIST
Salary: $30,000
Tax Rate: 30% ($750 per month)

Twice-monthly paychecks (taxes withheld): $875.00 each

Cash down payments available:
  House = $10,000; Auto = $7,000

— — — — — — — — — — — CUT APART — — — — — — — — — — —

3. DOCTOR
Salary: $65,000
Tax Rate: 30% ($1,895 per month)

Twice-monthly paychecks (taxes withheld): $1,760.83 each

Cash down payments available:
  House = $15,000; Auto = $8,000

— — — — — — — — — — — CUT APART — — — — — — — — — — —

4. CIVIL ENGINEER
Salary: $30,000
Tax Rate: 30% ($750 per month)

Twice-monthly paychecks (taxes withheld): $875.00 each

Cash down payments available:
  House = $10,000; Auto = $7,000

— — — — — — — — — — — CUT APART — — — — — — — — — — —

5. PLUMBER
Salary: $22,000
Tax Rate: 28% ($513 per month)

Twice-monthly paychecks (taxes withheld): $660.17 each

Cash down payments available:
  House = $10,000; Auto = $7,000

— — — — — — — — — — — CUT APART — — — — — — — — — — —

———————————— CUT APART ———————————

6. POSTAL WORKER
Salary: $23,000
Tax Rate: 28% ($537 per month)

Twice-monthly paychecks (taxes withheld): $689.83 each

Cash down payments available:
  House = $10,000; Auto = $7,000

———————————— CUT APART ———————————

7. AUTO ASSEMBLER
Salary: $23,000
Tax Rate: 28% ($537 per month)

Twice-monthly paychecks (taxes withheld): $689.83 each

Cash down payments available:
  House = $10,000; Auto = $7,000

———————————— CUT APART ———————————

8. NURSERY SCHOOL ADMINISTRATOR
Salary: $22,000
Tax Rate: 28% ($513 per month)

Twice-monthly paychecks (taxes withheld): $660.17 each

Cash down payments available:
  House = $10,000; Auto = $7,000

———————————— CUT APART ———————————

9. RETAIL SALESPERSON
Salary: $21,000
Tax Rate: 28% ($490 per month)

Twice-monthly paychecks (taxes withheld): $630.00 each

Cash down payments available:
  House = $10,000; Auto = $7,000

———————————— CUT APART ———————————

10. COLLEGE PROFESSOR
Salary: $23,000
Tax Rate: 28% ($537 per month)

Twice-monthly paychecks (taxes withheld): $689.83 each

Cash down payments available:
  House = $10,000; Auto = $7,000

———————————— CUT APART ———————————

— — — — — — — — — — — — CUT APART — — — — — — — — — — — —

11. ACCOUNTANT
Salary: $22,000
Tax Rate: 28% ($513 per month)

Twice-monthly paychecks (taxes withheld): $660.17 each

Cash down payments available:
  House = $10,000; Auto = $7,000

— — — — — — — — — — — CUT APART — — — — — — — — — — —

12. MEDICAL ASSISTANT
Salary: $21,000
Tax Rate: 28% ($490 per month)

Twice-monthly paychecks (taxes withheld): $630.00 each

Cash down payments available:
  House = $10,000; Auto = $7,000

— — — — — — — — — — — CUT APART — — — — — — — — — — —

13. NEWSPAPER REPORTER
Salary: $21,000
Tax Rate: 28% ($490 per month)

Twice-monthly paychecks (taxes withheld): $630.00 each

Cash down payments available:
  House = $10,000; Auto = $7,000

— — — — — — — — — — — CUT APART — — — — — — — — — — —

14. GROCERY STORE MANAGER
Salary: $26,000
Tax Rate: 28% ($650 per month)

Twice-monthly paychecks (taxes withheld): $758.33 each

Cash down payments available:
  House = $10,000; Auto = $7,000

— — — — — — — — — — — CUT APART — — — — — — — — — — —

15. CARPENTER
Salary: $23,000
Tax Rate: 28% ($537 per month)

Twice-monthly paychecks (taxes withheld): $689.83 each

Cash down payments available:
  House = $10,000; Auto = $7,000

— — — — — — — — — — — CUT APART — — — — — — — — — — —

— — — — — — — — — — — — — CUT APART — — — — — — — — — — —

16. ELECTRICIAN
Salary: $23,000
Tax Rate: 28% ($537 per month)

Twice-monthly paychecks (taxes withheld): $689.83 each

Cash down payments available:
  House = $10,000; Auto = $7,000

— — — — — — — — — — — — — CUT APART — — — — — — — — — — —

17. HIGH SCHOOL TEACHER
Salary: $18,000
Tax Rate: 24% ($360 per month)

Twice-monthly paychecks (taxes withheld): $570.00 each

Cash down payments available:
  House = $8,000; Auto = $6,000

— — — — — — — — — — — — — CUT APART — — — — — — — — — — —

18. AUTO MECHANIC
Salary: $17,000
Tax Rate: 24% ($340 per month)

Twice-monthly paychecks (taxes withheld): $538.33 each

Cash down payments available:
  House = $8,000; Auto = $6,000

— — — — — — — — — — — — — CUT APART — — — — — — — — — — —

19. SOCIAL WORKER
Salary: $19,000
Tax Rate: 24% ($380 per month)

Twice-monthly paychecks (taxes withheld): $601.67 each

Cash down payments available:
  House = $8,000; Auto = $6,000

— — — — — — — — — — — — — CUT APART — — — — — — — — — — —

20. RADIO ANNOUNCER
Salary: $16,000
Tax Rate: 24% ($320 per month)

Twice-monthly paychecks (taxes withheld): $506.67 each

Cash down payments available:
  House = $8,000; Auto = $6,000

— — — — — — — — — — — — — CUT APART — — — — — — — — — — —

Budget Percentage Guidelines

Below are the suggested *ranges* for each budget category.

Category	Percentage of NSI
3. Housing (Total)	30 — 36%
4. Food	12 — 17%
5. Auto (Total)	15 — 20%
6. Insurance	3 — 7%
7. Debts	5 — 6%
8. Entertainment	5 — 8%
9. Clothing	5 — 6%
10. Savings	5%
11. Medical Expenses	4 — 8%
12. Miscellaneous	5 — 10%

Division of Pay

PER YEAR $ _____   DIVISION OF PAY
PER MONTH $ _____   PER PAY PERIOD $ _____

MONTHLY PAYMENT CATEGORY	$_____ 1st PAY PERIOD	$_____ 2nd PAY PERIOD
1. Charitable Contributions		
2. Taxes		
NET SPENDABLE INCOME (PER MONTH)	$_____	$_____
3. Housing		
4. Food		
5. Automobile(s)		
6. Insurance		
7. Debts		
8. Enter. & Recreation		
9. Clothing		
10. Savings		
11. Medical		
12. Miscellaneous		
TOTALS (Items 3 through 12)	$_____	$_____

Individual Account Sheets

ACCOUNT NAME	MONTHLY ALLOCATION	1st PAY PERIOD	2nd PAY PERIOD

DATE	TRANSACTION	DEPOSIT		W/DRAW		BALANCE	

Steps in Budgeting

1. Select a job from Appendix A.

2. Determine your NSI.

3. Calculate your category limits on a copy of Form 1.

4. Select your budget needs from Appendix B.

5. Make sure income and expenses balance on Form 1.

6. Divide your expenses by pay period (Form 2).

7. Establish your individual accounts (Form 3).

8. Start a checking account ledger (Form 3).

9. Do one full month of business:
   - Record deposits on Form 4.
   - Record deposits in checkbook ledger and individual account sheets.
   - Write checks (Form 5) for all expenses.
   - Record expenditures in checkbook ledger and individual account sheets.

10. Balance your checkbook ledger, your budget and your bank statement.

11. Repeat steps 9 and 10 for additional months.

Installment Payments

First payment: 1/10 of initial loan ($1,000)   = $100

                        Plus 1% interest on balance   =   10

                        Payment   = $110

   Balance of loan $900

Second payment: 1/10 of initial loan ($1,000)   = $100

                        Plus 1% interest on balance   =   9

                        Payment   = $109

   Balance of loan $800

Third payment: 1/10 of initial loan ($1,000)   = $100

                        Plus 1% interest on balance   =   8

                        Payment   = $108

   Balance of loan $700

Fourth payment: 1/10 of initial loan ($1,000)   = $100

                        Plus 1% interest on balance   =   7

                        Payment   = $107

   Balance of loan $600

Etc.

Evaluating Life Insurance

1. How much do they need?

Present income	$24,000/yr
Survivors' income available	-11,000 (Social Security)
Additional income needed	$13,000

The additional income would come from investing the cash settlement of the life insurance policy.

$$\$13,000/\text{yr} \ 10\% = \$130,000$$

Therefore, a policy of $130,000 would be needed.

2. How much can they afford?

$15/mo is all they can afford since they also must purchase medical insurance.

3. What kind is best for them?

The only kind they can purchase is term insurance.

Comparing Term and Whole Life Insurance

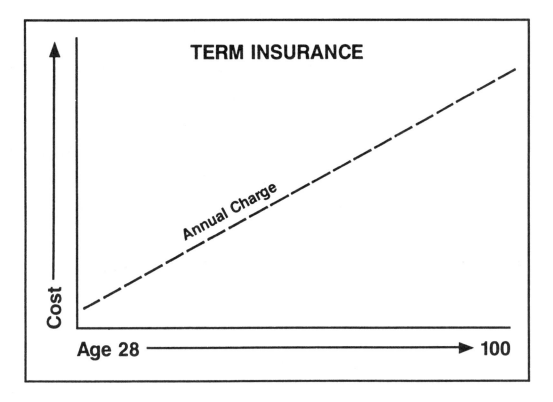

TERM INSURANCE

Annual Charge

Cost

Age 28 ———————————————————————▶ 100

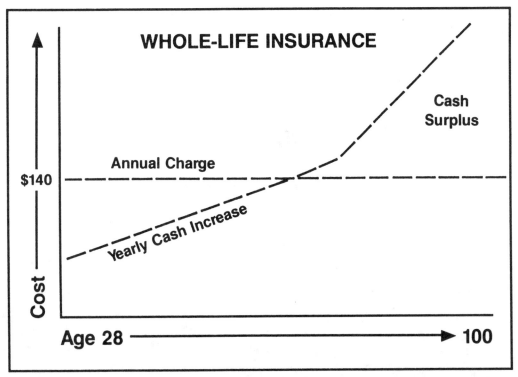

WHOLE-LIFE INSURANCE

Cash Surplus

Annual Charge

$140

Yearly Cash Increase

Cost

Age 28 ———————————————————————▶ 100

Adjustable Rate Mortgage

Definition: A mortgage loan where the annual interest rate can be changed according to a predetermined guide such as the "prime" interest rate.

Example: A thirty-year adjustable rate mortgage (ARM) for $100,000 beginning at 9 percent interest with a maximum yearly rate change of 1 percent and a total maximum rate change of 4.5 percent increase.

The Resume' Format

1. NAME:

   Name
   Complete Address
   Complete Phone Number

2. EDUCATION:

   Begin from your highest education and descend to your high school, listing:

   Name of school
   Address of the school
   Number of years you attended with the dates
   Year of graduation, degree and major

3. EXPERIENCE:

   List your work history in reverse chronological order.

   The company's name
   City
   A brief description of your position
   Any specific achievements, awards, inventions, etc.

4. OTHER EXPERIENCE OR ACTIVITIES:

   School, civic, and personal activities
   Hobbies of interest to an employer
   Awards
   Church, civic or school offices held

QUIZ ANSWERS

Lesson 3: 1—F, 2—T, 3—T, 4—B, 5—C.

Lesson 5: 1—F, 2—F, 3—T, 4—C, 5—D.

Lesson 6: 1—T, 2—F, 3—T, 4—C, 5—D.

Lesson 7: 1—F, 2—F, 3—F, 4—B, 5—D, 6—A, 7—C.
Note on Question 3—Most people need about ten times the income not provided through other sources.

Lesson 8: 1—F, 2—T, 3—T, 4—F, 5—T, 6—D, 7—B.

Lesson 9: 1—F, 2—T, 3—F, 4—F, 5—B, 6—C, 7—T, 8—A, 9—C.

Lesson 10: 1—F, 2—T, 3—F, 4—F, 5—T, 6—T, 7—C.

Lesson 12: 1—C, 2—I, 3—A, 4—G, 5—F, 6—T, 7—F, 8—F, 9—F, 10—T, 11—F, 12—A, 13—D, 14—B, 15—C.

Lesson 13: 1—F, 2—T, 3—F, 4—F, 5—T, 6—sacrificially, 7—C.